The American Revolution for Kids

The

American Revolution

for Kids

A History with 21 Activities

JANIS HERBERT

CHICAGO
REVIEW
PRESS

Library of Congress Cataloging-in-Publication Data

Herbert, Janis, 1956–
    The American Revolution for kids : a history with 21 activities / Janis Herbert.—1st ed.
     p.   cm.
    Summary: Discusses the events of the American Revolution, from the hated Stamp Act and the Boston Tea Party to the British surrender at Yorktown and the writing of the Constitution. Activities include making a tricorn hat and disovering local history.
  Includes bibliographical references (p. 135) and index.
    ISBN 1-55652-456-0
    1. United States—History—Revolution, 1775–1783—Juvenile literature. 2. United States—History—Revolution, 1775–1783—Study and teaching—Activity programs—Juvenile literature. [1. United States—History—Revolution, 1775–1783.] I. Title.
CURR E208 . H46 2002
973.3—dc21
                                                  2002007938

The author and the publisher disclaim all liability for use of information contained in this book.

Front cover: (top) portraits of Benjamin Franklin, John Hancock, Thomas Jefferson, and Samuel Adams courtesy of the National Archives and Records Administration; (center) painting "Washington at the Battle of Princeton" by Charles Willson Peale courtesy of The Art Museum, Princeton University, Princeton, N.J.; (middle left) "The Boston Massacre" by Paul Revere, (bottom center) "Join or Die" by Benjamin Franklin, (bottom right) painting "Burgoyne's Surrender at Saratoga" by Percy Moran courtesy of the Library of Congress; (bottom left) painting "The First Maryland Charging the British Guards" by Frank Buffmire and (middle right) drum carried by Luther Clark of North Carolina courtesy of Guildford Court House National Military Park.

Interior photos: pages 16–17, 19, 32, 66, 90, 112 (left) courtesy of North Wind Picture Archives. Pages 36, 50, 58, 59 courtesy of The Company of Military Historians. Pages 69 and 95 courtesy of Guilford Courthouse National Military Park. Page 112 (right) courtesy of Independence National Historical Park. Title page (middle and right); pages x, xviii, 1, 4, 8–11, 14, 20–21, 26–27, 30, 34, 35, 37–38, 41, 44–46, 48, 51–52, 54–55, 56–57, 61, 63, 65, 67–68, 72–74, 77–78, 81, 84, 87–89, 91–94, 98, 100, 103–104, 113, 117, 142 courtesy National Archives and Records Administration.

Cover design: Joan Sommers Design, Chicago
Interior design: Lindgren/Fuller Design

© 2002 by Janis Herbert
All rights reserved
First edition
Published by Chicago Review Press, Incorporated
814 North Franklin Street
Chicago, Illinois 60610
Printed in China by C & C Offset Company, Ltd.
5 4 3 2

For Sara and Marianne

Contents

Acknowledgments

W ITH THANKS TO National Park Service employees everywhere (especially Donald Long and Timothy Boyd, who went out of their way to help); Kent Fevurly and Larry Sanford for sharing their time and knowledge and for their excellent suggestions; Ruth and Don Ross, who once again came through with research and lots of support; Marianne Coogan, Sara Dickinson, Camillo Imbimbo, and Deborah Titus for their encouragement and ideas; Linda Matthews, Jaime Guthals, and Mark Voigt for efforts above and beyond; responsive and discerning editor Cynthia Sherry; designers Laura Lindgren and Celia Fuller for bringing the book to life; and Jeff—I can't thank you enough.

TIME LINE

1754–60	French and Indian War	**1774**	Coercive ("Intolerable") Acts and Quebec Act passed First Continental Congress meets
1760	George III becomes king of England	**1775**	Battles of Lexington and Concord (April 19) Second Continental Congress meets Washington appointed commander of Continental Army Battle of Bunker Hill (June 17) Defeat at Quebec (December 30)
1765	Stamp Act and Quartering Act passed Stamp Act Congress meets		
1766	Stamp Act repealed	**1776**	Thomas Paine writes *Common Sense* Siege of Boston ends Declaration of Independence signed (July 4) New York falls Battle of Trenton (December 25)
1767	Parliament passes Townshend Acts		
1768	British troops in Boston		
1770	Boston Massacre (March 5)	**1777**	Battle of Princeton (January 3) Fort Ticonderoga falls (July 6) **Battle of Bennington (August 16)** **Battle of Brandywine (September 11)** **Philadelphia falls (September 26)** **Battle of Germantown (October 6)**
1773	Parliament passes the Tea Act Boston Tea Party (December 16)		

Battle of Saratoga (October 7)
Burgoyne surrenders (October 17)
Congress passes Articles of Confederation (November 15)
Winter at Valley Forge

1778
France declares war
Battle of Monmouth Courthouse (June 28)
Savannah captured (December 29)

1779
George Rogers Clark captures Vincennes (February 25)
Bonhomme Richard vs. the *Serapis* (September 29)
Winter at Morristown, New Jersey

1780
Charleston falls (May 12)
Battle of Camden (August 16)
Battle of Kings Mountain (October 7)

1781
Battle of Cowpens (January 17)
Articles of Confederation adopted by states (March 1)
Battle of Guilford Courthouse (March 15)
Battle of Eutaw Springs (September 8)
Cornwallis surrenders at Yorktown (October 19)

1783
Treaty of Paris signed (September 3)
Continental Army disbanded; Washington retires

1786
Annapolis Convention
Shays's Rebellion

1787
Congress passes Northwest Ordinance
Constitutional Convention meets
Constitution signed (September 17)

1788
Constitution is ratified

1789
First meeting of Congress
George Washington sworn in as president,
     John Adams as vice president

1791
Congress adopts the Bill of Rights

Note to Readers

See the Glossary following Chapter 7 for definitions of unfamiliar words. Lists of officers who fought in the American and British armies and biographies of people mentioned in the text begin on page 121. For those interested in more information about the Revolutionary War and the American government, see Revolutionary War Sites to Visit, Web Sites to Explore, and the Bibliography at the back of the book.

"War's Begun"

IT SEEMED LIKE ANY OTHER DAY in the country schoolhouse on the outskirts of Boston. The youngest children pored over their primers, while older students recited Latin phrases. The schoolmaster looked sternly at those who wiggled or talked out of turn. Suddenly, a distant "tramp tramp tramp" broke the spring morning's stillness, and the students looked up from their books. The sound grew louder. Soon, to their amazement, hundreds of British soldiers marched past their school. The soldiers, dressed in crimson coats and tall red and gold hats, marched in step as their officers, mounted on magnificent horses, urged them forward. "Lay down your books," said the schoolmaster. "War's begun and school is done."

The British soldiers were marching against musket-toting American militiamen. The Americans, once loyal to the Crown, were preparing to fight for freedom from British rule. Over time, many of the colonists in British North America had become unhappy under Great Britain. They had raged against "Intolerable Acts" passed by Parliament and the royal proclamations that restricted their freedom. England's answer was to send troops and tighten its hold on the colonies. After years of protests and riots, the colonists and their mother country were at war.

At one time, such a war seemed impossible. The people living in the 13 colonies along the Atlantic coastline had long been loyal subjects of the English king. From the time of the earliest settlements in North America, they had considered themselves to be English and looked to their home country for guidance and support.

Only recently, the colonists and British soldiers had fought side by side against France and its Indian allies over France's North American

❖ Thirteen Colonies at a Glance ❖

The colonies Connecticut, Delaware, Georgia, Maryland, Massachusetts, New Hampshire, New Jersey, New York, North Carolina, Pennsylvania, Rhode Island, South Carolina, and Virginia

Milestones:

1585 Sir Walter Raleigh colonizes Roanoke Island (the settlers disappear without a trace)

1587 First English baby, Virginia Dare, born in North America

1607 London Company colonists and Captain John Smith found Jamestown, Virginia

1619 First representative assembly in America meets in Jamestown; slaves brought to Virginia

1620 Pilgrims land at Plymouth Rock to build a community based on their Mayflower Compact

1626 New Amsterdam (Manhattan) bought from Indians by Dutch West India Company for 24 dollars' worth of beads

1634 Catholics find a welcome home in Lord Baltimore's Maryland colony

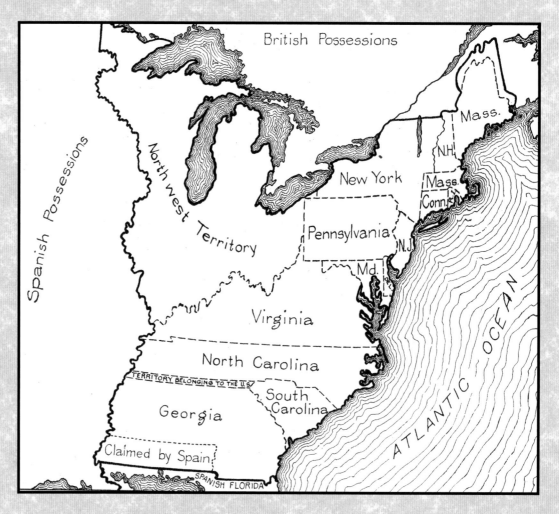

1636 Providence (Rhode Island), founded by Roger Williams, becomes known for religious tolerance

1638 Swedish settlements built along the Delaware River

1639 "Fundamental Orders" (an early constitution) written by settlers of Connecticut

1663 Royal charter granted to colonize the Carolinas (North and South Carolina officially separate in 1729)

1664 The Dutch surrender New Netherland colony to the English (it is divided into New York and New Jersey)

1679 New Hampshire, once part of Massachusetts, becomes a colony

1682 Quaker William Penn founds the city of Philadelphia (Pennsylvania colony)

1733 The last colony, Georgia, becomes home to English debtors and dissenters

Population in 1770 Over two million

Biggest city in 1770 Philadelphia, population about 34,000

Ethnicity African, Dutch, English, French, German, Irish, Scandinavian, and Scottish. Most were English; Africans, brought to the colonies as slaves, were the second-largest group.

Occupations and industry Southerners raised rice, sugar, tobacco, and indigo on large plantations. The New England economy was based on fishing and shipbuilding. In the prosperous middle colonies farmers raised wheat, vegetables, and fruit, while craftsmen made furniture, shoes, and glass.

Religions Anglican, Baptist, Catholic, Congregationalist, Jewish, Lutheran, and Quaker. Many came to the colonies seeking religious freedom.

Government Under British rule. Most colonies had a royal governor appointed by the king. Local governing bodies, such as Virginia's House of Burgesses, were based on Britain's Parliament. Half of their members were appointed by the king and half elected by colonial land-owners. The king regarded the laws they passed to be subject to his will and to Parliament.

Favorite beverage Tea!

claims. (Indian warriors preferred the French, who bought their furs, to the English colonists, who settled on their land.) Fierce battles raged in the western forests and mountains, and north into Canada. The British were victorious against their longtime French enemies, and France was driven off the continent.

The colonists celebrated that victory with bonfires and parades. With the French gone, they saw their future in the lands to the west. They began to make plans for new settlements. Their British ruler wasn't so sure. It would be a lot of trouble to hold those lands against the Indians who lived there. When the Ottawa Indian chief Pontiac led his warriors against English forts in the west, the king threw up his hands. It wasn't worth sending more soldiers across the ocean to fight for those lands. He set a boundary at the Appalachian Mountains, where the colonies should end. The colonists were disappointed that they wouldn't be able to expand to new settlements and wondered why they had bothered to help fight the French at all.

This was not ancient history to the schoolchildren. Their fathers had fought in the French and Indian War. They knew, too, that the war had created problems between Great Britain and its American colonies. The British government was deeply in debt from the French and Indian War. The colonists, Parliament had decided, would have to pay.

The American Revolution for Kids

George III

Boston Tea Party

one

Sons and Daughters of Liberty

1760: Be a King!

"Be a king, George!" demanded Queen Augusta. She wanted her son to be a powerful ruler. The last two kings of Great Britain, George I and George II, were from German royal families and didn't really care what happened in England or its colonies. They left most of the decisions up to the prime minister and Parliament. When George III took the throne, he remembered his mother's words. He intended to be a strong ruler.

In some countries kings were all-powerful, but in Great Britain there were limits on the king's rule. George III found this very frustrating. Over the centuries of England's history, the monarchy had gradually been forced to give up some of its power. The nobles, knights, and burgesses (leading citizens) of England had gained rights and a voice in their government. Eventu-

ally they had an official role in the state and became part of the governing body known as Parliament.

He wasn't cruel, but George III did not intend to be pushed around. He was king! That pesky Parliament, for instance—he couldn't just do away with it, but he threatened or rewarded its members until they voted his way. And those upstart colonists across the ocean? King George was not about to let them decide for themselves on important issues such as trade and taxes. The colonies existed to benefit the Crown! Their trade and markets were supposed to bring wealth and power to Great Britain.

Deciding for themselves was exactly what many colonists wanted to do. They worked hard to build towns and settlements in a wild new land. They fought, often without any help from the British, to keep their settlements safe from Indian

1

attacks. They built up industries and trade and added to the wealth of their mother country. Yet the distant government seemed only to care about how much money it could make off its colonies. Since George III had come to the throne, the colonists felt things had gotten worse.

As far back as the 1660s, Parliament had passed laws telling the colonists exactly what, and with whom, they could trade. The Navigation Acts forbade the colonists to sell certain goods to any country other than England. In another act, Parliament demanded that any goods the colonists bought from other countries had to go through England first so a special tax could be collected on them. Parliament even put a stop to some kinds of trade among the colonies. England passed these acts so its own merchants and land-owners would profit. The colonists seethed with anger. They filled their ships with illegal goods and smuggled them past customs agents to avoid the trade laws they felt were so unjust.

George III stamped his royal foot. He would bring a stop to this smuggling! He intended to control all the trade going in and out of the colonies. He armed his customs officials in colonial ports such as Boston and New York with "writs of assistance." These documents allowed them to enter any buildings, at any time, to search for illegal smuggled goods. The colonists cried, "Unfair!" In England, such writs were illegal. There, not even King George could enter a man's home without going through the legal system. The colonists who had left England to settle in North America had been assured that they and their

✤ The King and the Kingdom ✤

George III was a tall, gray-eyed 22-year-old when he was crowned King of England. He inherited the throne from his grandfather, George II. All three Georges were from the royal House of Hanover (a region of Germany). For a time, the kings of England didn't even speak English! During his reign, George III founded the Royal Academy of Arts, collected tens of thousands of books for his royal library, fathered 15 children, and lost the American colonies. George loved gardening and farming (people called him "Farmer George"—behind his back, of course). After he began to show signs of mental illness, he was declared unfit to rule. His eldest son carried out his duties as king.

George III's 60-year reign was the second longest in British history. He was the most recent king in a monarchy that stretched back to the warrior-chieftains of the Dark Ages. He shared power with England's Parliament.

Made up of the king, the House of Commons, and the House of Lords, Parliament made laws for Great Britain and its colonies. In ancient times, the House of Lords was a group of noblemen who counseled the king. Membership in this group became hereditary. The House of Commons first met in the 13th century, when knights and burgesses were summoned to meet with the king. In spite of the name, this body did not really speak for the common people. In the 1700s, only nobles and wealthy landowners were represented in Parliament.

Several prime ministers (leaders of Parliament appointed by the king) served during George III's reign. King George forced William Pitt, who sided with the colonists, to resign but later brought him back to power. George Grenville led Parliament to pass the Stamp Act. Lord North held the office for years and completely supported King George and his policies.

heirs would have all the rights of free English subjects. What had happened to that promise?

Some colonists claimed the writs of assistance went against their "natural rights." Natural rights were so basic, they said, that they went beyond Parliament's laws or King George's decrees. Preachers in pulpits and street-corner philosophers quoted the philosopher John Locke, who wrote

"Sign Right Here, King"

King John of England was so broke he was nicknamed "Lackland." He lost money in a war against France and tried to get more by taxing his barons. They marched on London in protest and presented the king with a list of their own demands. At Runnymede Meadow, King John agreed to the demands, signed the parchment, and affixed it with his royal seal. From that day in June 1215 on, John and all the future kings of England were bound by this document, called the "Magna Carta" ("Great Charter").

The Magna Carta limited the king's power, especially his power to tax his subjects. It also stated that "no freeman shall be imprisoned except by the lawful judgment of his peers" (thus, trial by jury had been created). The Magna Carta stated that these laws of the land were supreme, and even the king must obey them. Copies were made and read to subjects in all corners of the kingdom.

In the 1600s, English kings signed a "Petition of Rights" and a "Bill of Rights." They promised not to tax without consent, imprison without cause, quarter (house) soldiers in the homes of English subjects, or interfere with free speech in Parliament.

❖

that it was a "law of nature" that all people have an equal right to life, liberty, and property. Locke also said that the purpose of government was to protect these rights. The colonists thought that since their government was breaking these ancient (though unwritten) laws, that gave them the right to refuse to obey the writs of assistance. King George said, "We do not agree."

The Parson's Tobacco

A lawsuit in Virginia became the talk of the colonies. It was about a parson and his tobacco, but it was also about whether England had the right to overrule local laws passed by the colonies.

Virginia's clergymen were paid in tobacco, 17,000 pounds of it a year. During bad crop years, the price of tobacco was high and the clergymen made a lot of extra money. Planters and Virginia's colonial House of Burgesses thought it would be better if the clergymen were paid with money instead. The House of Burgesses passed a law to this effect.

Unhappy clergymen took this matter up with the British government, which struck down the Virginia law. When they still didn't get their tobacco, one of them took the matter to court. The case, called the "Parson's Cause," became famous. So did Patrick Henry, the intense, red-headed lawyer opposing the parson. Henry stood in the Virginia courtroom and passionately argued that the British government could not cancel the colony's law. The jury agreed and gave the parson only a penny for his trouble. A struggle for power between England and its colonies had begun.

The acts passed by the distant Parliament affected the colonists' livelihoods and their everyday lives, yet they had no vote or voice. When they complained, the king responded by sending soldiers across the ocean. The colonists felt threatened when they saw the armed, red-coated soldiers in their towns. When they needed help, the colonists said, they were left on their own. Now, British soldiers were everywhere.

1765: Tyranny!

England had many debts to pay after the French and Indian War, and the members of Parliament felt it was only right that the colonists pay them. After all, British troops had driven the French off their colonial doorstep. The colonists disagreed. More than 20,000 of them had fought in that war, too, and they had their own debts to pay. Besides, England and France had been fighting for 70 years, not only in America but in Europe and Africa, too. England was lucky to have the colonists to help them beat their longtime enemy.

Parliament tried different ways to get money from the colonies. It passed a "Sugar Act," to make money off the profitable trade in sugar and molasses, and a "Currency Act," which prevented colonists from using their own paper money

Come join Hand in Hand, brave AMERICANS all,
And rouse your bold Hearts at fair LIBERTY's Call.

—FROM "THE LIBERTY SONG," BY JOHN DICKINSON

(it wasn't worth as much to British merchants). When it passed the "Stamp Act," the colonists howled in anger.

This new law stated that all official papers in the colonies must be stamped by a government agent—for a fee. This meant that people had to pay for special stamps for all court documents, diplomas, wills, and licenses. There were even stamps for newspapers, almanacs, and playing cards!

Everyone was upset about the Stamp Act. How was it that Parliament, 3,000 miles away, had the right to lay such a heavy burden on the people of the colonies? From New Hampshire to Georgia, people were angry because they had no say about what happened to them. They had no representatives in Parliament who would stand up and state their point of view. The English landowners were represented. Why shouldn't the colonists have a voice in their government, too? Massachusetts lawyer James Otis, who had already been fighting in court against the writs of assistance, coined a phrase that colonists everywhere repeated: "Taxation without representation is tyranny!"

The Stamp Act was quickly followed by the "Quartering Act." This law decreed that colonists had to pay for the British soldiers stationed in the colonies. Soldiers could be quartered in the homes of families, whether the families wanted them there or not. The British government said the law was necessary because there wasn't enough housing for its soldiers. This new act was threatening. With soldiers lodged in their shops and homes, who would dare challenge any acts of Parliament or the king?

1765: Rabble-Rousing

Samuel Adams knew how to make his voice heard (maybe because he was one of 12 children). His father, a Massachusetts brewer, paid Samuel's university tuition in flour and molasses, then sent him to apprentice with a successful trader. But Samuel Adams had no head for business or brewing; his passion was for politics. When Parliament passed the Stamp Act, he went into action. He sought out the common people, spending time at the docks and taverns to listen to their opinions and share his own. The British thought he was a nuisance and a rabble-rouser and kept an eye out for the determined man in his rumpled red cloak.

Many of the people Samuel Adams met felt as he did, that the new acts passed by Parliament

Samuel Adams
(1722–1803)

There might not have been a revolution without Samuel Adams. He persuaded and pushed his fellow colonists to action. He was a founder of the Sons of Liberty, a representative at the Continental Congresses, and a signer of the Declaration of Independence. After the war, he was governor of Massachusetts.

❖

Brew a Batch of Root Beer

If Samuel Adams had stuck to brewing, Americans might be singing "God Save the King" instead of "The Star-Spangled Banner." Make this brew for Independence Day and make a toast to Samuel Adams!

What you need
Small bowl
1 teaspoon dry yeast
½ cup warm water
Stirring spoon
2 cups sugar
5 teaspoons root beer extract (available in the spice aisle of your local super-

market or from a home brewing supply company)
Gallon jug with lid
8 cups hot water

In a small bowl, stir the yeast in the warm water until it dissolves. Pour the sugar, yeast mixture, and root beer extract into the jug. Add the hot water, put the lid on the jar, and shake until the ingredients are mixed. Set the jug in a sunny window and let the mixture rest for several hours, then put it in the refrigerator until it is cold. Drink it the next day.

violated their rights. They were angry and felt helpless, but after talking to Adams they didn't feel so helpless anymore. He organized protests to get the colonists' message back to England. They were not going to pay!

Boston was in turmoil, and much of it was due to Samuel Adams. He helped to form a secret society pledged to fight the Stamp Act. They called themselves the "Sons of Liberty," taking their name from a phrase coined by Parliament's Isaac Barré, who had voted against the Stamp

Act. Barré warned that the Stamp Act would lead the colonists, those "sons of liberty," to revolt against their mother country. The Sons of Liberty got support from John Hancock, the richest man in New England.

The "Liberty Tree," a large elm tree in a central part of Boston, became their favorite place to gather and talk. British officials shivered when their carriages passed the Liberty Tree. Its trunk was covered with flyers protesting the Stamp Act. Dummies dressed like the British officials hung

I Protest!

There are many things that need fixing in the world and lots of ways to make your voice heard. While some colonists used violence to protest the Stamp Act, others challenged it by writing and boycotting. Women calling themselves the "Daughters of Liberty" boycotted British goods. This meant they and their families had to work a lot harder to make everything themselves. It was a sign of support for the colonial cause to wear homespun clothes. To bring attention to the cause, women brought their spinning wheels to village squares and held spinning contests.

Since the American Revolution, there have been other struggles for freedom and equality. During the 1960s Civil Rights movement, Martin Luther King, Jr., preached and led marches in his fight for racial equality. India's Mahatma Gandhi used passive resistance (such as fasting, sitting, and walking) to gain his country's freedom and to foster change. They taught us new ways to protest.

Is there an issue you want to see changed? Here are some ways you can do your part.

- **Boycott!** Refuse to use products that harm animals or the environment. Ask others to join you.
- **Write!** Tell your government what matters to you. Enlist your classmates to do the same and start an e-mail or letter-writing campaign. Publish articles about important issues in your school's newspaper. Write letters to the editor of your hometown paper.
- **Create!** Compose and perform a protest song. Make a photo journal that exposes a problem. Write a story—Upton Sinclair's *The Jungle* led to reforms in the meat-packing industry; Harriet Beecher Stowe's *Uncle Tom's Cabin* roused people against slavery.

Can you think of more ways to protest? Gather your friends and meet under your own Liberty Tree (better yet—plant one!) to come up with creative, nonviolent ways to make your voice heard.

---

from the tree's branches. When Sons of Liberty groups began to form in other towns, they met beneath other "liberty trees" or raised "liberty poles" and held noisy gatherings around them.

To protest the Stamp Act, many colonists boycotted (refused to buy) British goods. The Sons of Liberty turned to violence to get their way. They threatened merchants who traded with England. They destroyed the homes of British government agents. By the time the Stamp Act was about to go into effect, there wasn't a person in the colonies who would serve as a stamp agent.

Lawyer James Otis wrote to influential men in every colony, inviting them to send delegates to meet and discuss the Stamp Act. Representatives from nine of the colonies met in New York. (The other four supported the idea but didn't choose their delegates in time.) This meeting, called the "Stamp Act Congress," was the first time the colonies had worked together in a common cause. Before this time, they acted as if they were 13 separate countries. Now they had a common goal. A Massachusetts delegate, Dr. Joseph Warren, noticed it. "Until now the colonies were foolishly jealous of each other. Now they are united," he said. As allies, they would be more powerful.

The delegates were angry about the Stamp Act, but most wanted to remain part of Great Britain. Most of the people in the colonies felt the same way. Though they were angry, few thought about breaking away from England. They simply wanted to have their voices heard. John Dickinson, a delegate from Pennsylvania, wrote a declaration to King George and Parliament denying their right to tax the colonies without consent. The Stamp Act Congress sent the declaration to England.

King George and the members of Parliament already knew how the colonists felt. The boycotts were hurting British merchants. An American visitor in London, Benjamin Franklin, was questioned by members of Parliament about the situation. "What was the temper of America towards Great Britain before the Stamp Act?" he was asked. "The best in the world," Franklin said. "And now?" they asked. "Oh, very much altered!" he said. He told Parliament that the colonists would not pay unless "compelled by force of arms."

When the hated Stamp Act was about to go into effect, the Sons of Liberty planned special demonstrations. Merchants shut down their businesses. People pretended to be in mourning, tolling bells and flying flags at half-mast. In one city, a funeral was held. On the coffin, the word *Liberty* made clear what had died. The riots, boycotts, and declarations were heard across the ocean. Parliament canceled the Stamp Act.

When the news reached the colonies, people rejoiced. They sang and danced in the streets. They gathered around huge bonfires and cheered for their kinsmen across the ocean. The king was on their side after all! Feelings of loyalty swelled their hearts. They celebrated King George's birthday with festivals and banquets. Statues of the king were unveiled in town squares.

1767: Champagne Charlie and the Tax on Tea

The colonists had celebrated too soon. The Stamp Act was canceled, but, at the same time, Parliament passed a new law, the "Declaratory Act." With this law, Britain held on to its right to tax the colonies without their consent. Soon it did.

Britain's Chancellor of the Exchequer (treasury), Charles Townshend, wasn't about to give up on taxing the colonies. One day, after a few glasses of champagne, he stood up and gave a speech in Parliament. He scolded the members for taking back the Stamp Act. When one of them replied that they didn't dare tax the colonists, he boasted, "I will!"

With his urging, Parliament passed the "Townshend Acts," which required the colonists to pay taxes on glass, lead, paper, and tea. British customs agents used their writs of assistance to enter buildings and board ships to make sure these goods weren't being smuggled into American

John Hancock
(1737 – 1793)

John Hancock did everything in a big way. He spent money lavishly, wore lavender suits of silk and satin, and signed his name with a flourish. Heads turned when his bright yellow carriage clattered down Boston streets. He was one of the richest men in the colonies, though his father had been a modest clergyman. John inherited his fortune from a wealthy uncle and took over his uncle's trading (and smuggling) empire. As president of the Second Continental Congress, John Hancock was the first to sign the Declaration of Independence. He became governor of Massachusetts and served nine terms.

❖

ports. Samuel Adams and the Sons of Liberty went back to making the British agents miserable. Once again, colonists boycotted British goods.

In New York, General Thomas Gage, the commander in chief of British troops in America, was having a difficult time. No one would help him find homes for his soldiers. The colonists refused to obey the Quartering Act. General Gage took his problem to the colony's government, the New York Assembly, but it would not force people to open their homes. Gage had the British royal governor of New York dissolve the Assembly. The colonists were outraged. Were they to have no government of their own? British soldiers pulled down a liberty pole in New York and cut it into little pieces to show their scorn. People rioted in the streets.

In the harbor of Boston, British customs officials seized a ship, the *Liberty*, which they suspected of carrying smuggled goods. It belonged to John Hancock, the wealthy merchant behind the Sons of Liberty. The Sons of Liberty rioted and set fires. British customs agents feared for their lives.

Great Britain reacted to the riots by ordering two regiments of troops to Boston. British ships, bristling with cannons, soon filled Boston's harbor. British soldiers paraded in the streets. Parliament had ordered them to find the troublemakers and bring them back to England for trial and punishment.

With British troops in their streets and buildings, Bostonians were tense. They taunted the soldiers, calling them "redcoats" and "lobsterbacks"

British cartoon of Bostonians tarring and feathering the tax man

for their crimson-red uniforms. Night after night, fights broke out between soldiers and citizens. One involved the lawyer James Otis. An argument with a British customs agent turned into a brawl, and Otis was beaten by British soldiers. He never quite recovered from a blow he received on the head.

One cold night in March 1770, a British soldier standing guard at a Boston customs house became the target of a crowd of angry people. They jeered and threw snowballs at him until he called for help. His captain sent soldiers to get him away from the crowd, giving them strict orders to hold their fire. When they arrived, the scene was chaotic. People threw rocks and dared them to "Fire!" One private shot his musket, then the rest began to shoot. Crispus Attucks, a black sailor and former slave, was the first in the crowd to fall. Five people were killed in the incident, which became known as the "Boston Massacre."

As bad as the incident was, public opinion made it seem even worse. It was said all over Boston that the soldiers had fired in cold blood and without cause. They were brought to trial for murder.

One of the lawyers arguing for the soldiers was John Adams. Adams was a patriot, but when asked to represent the soldiers, he took the job. He thought the law and a fair trial were more important than his own opinions or politics. He argued so well that the Boston jury found the soldiers not guilty of the charge.

Parliament withdrew most of the Townshend Acts. But it kept the tax on tea to prove that England still had the right to tax the colonies. British troops were temporarily removed from Boston, and things settled down for a time. Still, there were ugly feelings between the colonists and Britain. These feelings erupted when a British patrol ship, the *Gaspee,* ran aground while chasing a smuggler in the waters off Rhode Island. A mob gathered, pulled the sailors off the ship's

Patriots (Whigs) vs. Loyalists (Tories)

Not all the colonists felt the same way. While many people protested against the British government, many others (from one-fifth to one-third of the colonists) remained firmly loyal to the king. Those who rebelled and fought against England became known as "patriots" or "Whigs." Those loyal to the crown were called "loyalists" or "Tories." (The words *Whig* and *Tory* came from the names of political parties in Great Britain.) Even some patriots didn't want to completely break away from British rule. As relations grew tense between the colonies and Great Britain, it caused fierce divisions among neighbors, friends, and family members.

The Boston Massacre

Friends! Brethren! Countrymen!
The detested TEA is in the harbor and
tyranny stares you in the face!

deck, and set it on fire. The king offered a huge reward for the capture of those involved. Any who were caught, he decreed, would be brought to England for trial. No one came forward to tell. They felt that no rebellious colonist would receive a fair trial in England.

Samuel Adams and Joseph Warren saw the incident as a chance to unite the colonies against their mother country. They formed "committees of correspondence" to keep patriots in all the colonies in touch with each other. Horseback riders carried their messages from town to town. If a time came when action was necessary, they would all be ready.

1773: A Tea Party

The English East India Company held many tons of tea in its warehouses, but the tea needed to be sold soon or the company would go bankrupt. Rather than see the company go under, Parliament passed the "Tea Act." The East India Company would be the only company allowed to sell tea in the American colonies. Their tea would have a market, Parliament would collect the tax on it, and everyone would be happy.

Everyone, that is, except the colonists. Parliament had found another way to tax them without their consent. The tea was cheap, but that did not tempt them to betray their principles. The committees of correspondence made their plans. They intended to stop the East India Company from bringing tea into colonial ports.

When a ship landed in Charleston (South Carolina colony), the tea was unloaded and left to rot in damp warehouses. Philadelphia colonists refused to let an East India ship even enter their port. In New York, a storm sent a tea-laden ship back to sea and saved colonists the trouble. When three East India Company ships brought tea to Boston's harbor, Bostonians fumed, then held a noisy town meeting. They voted unanimously that the tea should be sent back to England. Then they posted guards to make sure the cargo wasn't unloaded from the ships.

At a second town meeting, Thomas Hutchinson, the British royal governor of Massachusetts, said he would not allow the ships to sail back to England without unloading their cargoes. He refused to be bullied by the angry townspeople. Samuel Adams stood up and left the meeting, the Sons of Liberty rallying behind him. "This meeting can do nothing more to save the country!" he declared.

John Adams
(1735–1826)

Young John Adams hated studying. He told his father, who came up with a solution. "If your studies don't suit you," his father said, "my meadow yonder needs a ditch." After two days of digging, John was happy to go back to his books. When he grew up, he became a lawyer. During the Stamp Act crisis, he wrote brilliant and inspiring essays about rights and government. Adams served as a delegate to the Continental Congresses, then as a diplomat who settled the peace treaty with Britain. He became vice president under George Washington and the second president of the United States. John Adams (who was a cousin to Samuel Adams) and his wife, Abigail, had four children. One of them, John Quincy Adams, became the nation's sixth president.

Rally Mohawks!
Bring out your axes,
And tell King George, we'll pay no taxes!

That night, the Sons of Liberty smeared their faces with grease and soot and dressed up like Mohawk Indians. No one dared stop them as they boarded the ships with axes over their shoulders. They chopped up every crate of tea in the ships' holds and dumped the contents into the Boston Harbor. The incident quickly became known as the "Boston Tea Party."

The men didn't disturb anything else on the ships. When they were done, they marched quietly back to their homes. John Adams thought the Tea Party was a dignified and daring protest. King George saw it as revolt. He said, "We must master the colonies or totally leave them alone."

★ ★

ACTIVITY

Liberty Tea Punch

Tea was by far the most popular drink in the colonies. Hardly anyone drank coffee, and most people thought plain water was bad for their health. When the colonists boycotted their favorite beverage, they learned to make tea from raspberry, blackberry, and currant leaves and sage. Try making this revolutionary punch.

What you need
4 cups water
Pot
2 bags raspberry tea
Pitcher
2 cups ginger ale
Ice
Glasses
Mint leaves

Bring the water to a boil in the pot. Steep the tea in the boiling water for 5 minutes. Allow the tea to cool, then pour it into the pitcher. Add the ginger ale. Serve over ice, with a mint leaf in each glass.

★ ★

1774: "Intolerable Acts"

Parliament quickly ordered the port of Boston closed. No ship could leave or bring goods into port until its residents paid for the tea they'd destroyed. Boston could starve! Next, Parliament dissolved the government of the Massachusetts colony (they continued to meet in secret). King George ordered General Thomas Gage to stop Boston's town meetings and send lawbreakers to England for trial. The Quartering Act was revived in all of the colonies. Parliament called these actions the "Coercive Acts." The colonists named them "Intolerable Acts" and rose in protest against them.

At the same time, Parliament passed the "Quebec Act," which extended Canada's border far to the south, into land claimed by other colonies. Now their territory was being taken away as well.

General Gage occupied Boston with 15 regiments of soldiers. They camped and drilled in Boston's Common. Patriots in all the colonies felt as threatened as the citizens of Boston. Would their turn be next?

The Virginia House of Burgesses was soon dissolved, too, but its members (including Patrick Henry and another redhead, Thomas Jefferson) met at an inn to talk. They agreed that an attack on Massachusetts was an attack on all the colonies. They sent messages through their committees of correspondence to leaders in each colony. It was time to unite.

two

Who Were the Colonists?

Tinkers, Tailors, Candlestick Makers

The English thought of the colonies as 13 wayward children disobeying their mother country. For decades, the colonists had been happy to be the children of England, but now they felt they were grown up and ready to do things their own way. They had proved, by settling in the wild new land and building thriving communities, that they could do things on their own. In their struggles, they had developed a habit of independence.

Day-to-day life in 18th-century America encouraged this habit. Most people were farmers who raised their food and made their own clothes and furnishings. They had no plumbing; they dug wells for their water. They had no electricity but made candles for light and chopped wood

We have an old Mother that peevish is grown,
She snubs us like Children that scarce walk alone.
She forgets we're grown up and have sense of our own;
Which nobody can deny!

—A POEM BY BENJAMIN FRANKLIN

Faneuil Hall, Boston

to heat their homes. They hunted and fished, plowed and planted, built houses and barns. When people became sick, they were treated with home remedies.

Young Massachusetts boys signed on as sailors to fish the open seas or trade in far-off lands. In the southernmost colony, the wild frontier land of Georgia, sturdy pioneer families worked together to build cabins and clear dense forests. In small towns across the colonies, blacksmiths, tanners, glassmakers, coopers, cobblers, and tailors labored. Women washed and cooked, spun and sewed, milked cows, made butter and cheese, slaughtered animals, tended their gardens, and then asked, "What else is there to do?"

Children had chores too. In the morning, boys were roused out of bed early to bring in firewood. If the fire went out during the night, they would run to a neighbor's home to borrow hot coals. They hauled heavy wooden buckets up from the well and carried water to the house. They watered and fed the livestock. Girls prepared breakfast, fed the chickens and gathered their eggs, and helped look after younger siblings. After a few hours at school (if they were lucky enough to attend), boys and girls would come back to weed the garden, gather vegetables, pick berries, and shell corn. Girls spun wool, sewed, and cooked while their brothers chopped wood.

Many communities had schools, but not everyone attended, or they did so for just a short time. Boys were needed on the farm to help during harvest and other busy seasons. Some people

Old-time school in Pennsylvania

thought it wasn't important for girls to know more than the basics of reading and writing, so many girls didn't attend school at all. A few went to special girls' schools where they learned to sew and embroider, dance and sing.

Some children walked long miles to school. Others came by wagon, pulled by an old horse that could be spared from farm work. In the South, where there were fewer towns and people lived far apart from each other, it was more

A Sampler

Colonial girls made samplers (pieces of cloth decorated with needlework) to practice sewing and embroidering. They stitched their ABCs, simple designs, or homey sayings such as "Whistling Girls and Crowing Hens Never Come to a Very Good End." Try making a sampler of your own.

What you need

Cloth

Scissors

Pencil

Embroidery needle

Embroidery thread in different colors

Cut the cloth into a square or rectangle. Draw a simple design or saying on the cloth with the pencil. Thread the needle and knot the end of the thread. Outline your letters or design with the thread, using one or more of the types of stitches shown here.

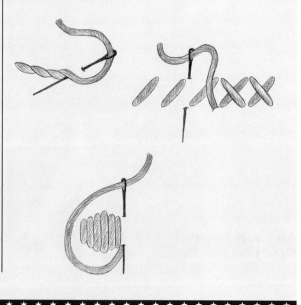

common for wealthy families to have their children tutored at home or to send them to live with a teacher (usually a local clergyman).

When the boys entered their one-room schoolhouse, they removed their caps and bowed to the teacher. Girls curtsied. If another adult entered the room, they all stood up. Discipline was very strict. Unruly boys were whipped with birch rods or thumped on the head with thimbles.

Students who fought might be yoked (joined) together for a day.

The children sat on long wooden benches, and their schoolmaster called on one grade at a time to stand and recite their lessons. While they did, the others read (always out loud—the noise was deafening) or practiced their penmanship. The students wrote "ciphers" (addition and subtraction problems) with slate pencils or goose quill pens. Their ink was made from powdered pigment or from tree bark steeped like tea.

Young pupils studied from *The New England Primer*, a book of alphabet rhymes, pictures, and prayers that was used everywhere in the colonies. The book set its lessons in rhyme to help young pupils remember them more easily. "M!" they shouted together. "The Moon gives light in time of night. N! Nightingales sing in time of spring." To learn the number of days in each month, they sang:

Thirty days hath September, April, June,
    and November.
All the rest have thirty-one
Excepting February alone;
Which hath but twenty-eight, in fine,
Till leap year gives it twenty-nine.

Boys from the upper classes were very well educated. They were expected to know Latin and Greek, ancient history, geometry and trigonometry, surveying, navigation, and more. A lucky few went on to college, either to one of the few colleges in the colonies or across the ocean to an English school.

It was common for boys to attend school only until age 13, then become apprenticed to a craftsman to learn a trade. As an apprentice, a boy helped with the easiest menial chores until he learned some skills. In a few years, after learning the trade, he became a journeyman, working under the supervision of the master craftsman. A boy might become a cooper (who made casks and barrels), a tanner (who turned hides into leather), a tailor, a cobbler, or a joiner (who made cabinets). Blacksmiths were in demand because they made tools, nails, and horseshoes. Silversmiths, like Paul Revere, made tea sets and tableware.

When people came to town in their horse-drawn wagons, they visited the cobbler to have a pair of shoes made and bought crocks and plates from the potter, who shaped his products on his revolving potter's wheel. Other craftsmen brought their trade to their customers. Chandlers traveled from one farmhouse to another carrying molds and tools to make candles and soap. Tinkers came knocking once a year to mend pots and kettles. These wandering craftsmen were welcomed for their skills and the news and gossip they brought with them.

"Ordinary" and Everyday Life

Of course, there was no television or radio. There weren't many newspapers or books. News traveled slowly—and people did, too. (When John Adams left Boston for Philadelphia, the trip took him two weeks.) Roads and bridges were few, making travel difficult. People walked, rode horses, or bounced along rough dirt roads in coaches. In the winter, they bundled up and traveled by sleigh. Travelers crossed rivers on

Abigail Adams
(1744–1818)

At a time when girls were expected to devote their lives to childrearing and chores, Abigail Smith had something else in mind. She spent her childhood reading the books in her father's library. Her lively mind attracted John Adams, and they married. When her husband was selected as a delegate to the Continental Congress, Abigail managed the house and farm while raising and educating their four children. She wrote her husband long letters about her life and ideas. Though it was thought unseemly for a woman to show an interest in politics, Abigail spoke her mind, sometimes signing her letters "Sister Delegate." As her husband worked to shape a new nation, she reminded him that women should have political rights and spoke out against slavery. Her ideas greatly influenced her husband, her "Dearest Friend," who became the second president of the United States.

flat ferryboats while their horses swam behind them. Before a postal system was organized, people sent mail by trusting their letters to passing travelers. These were the days before houses were numbered; writers addressed the envelopes with descriptions, such as "Sarah Goodfriend, north of the sign of the Copper Kettle and opposite the town pump."

Later, post riders carried mail and newspapers from town to town, changing their horses at inns (called "ordinaries" in those days) along the way. The village ordinary served as a place for travelers to rest and as a meeting place for local people. When the post rider came to town, everyone gathered at the ordinary to hear the latest news. The news wasn't always fresh. It could take weeks for information to get from one colony to another. Travelers and news coming from England took more than a month. When post riders brought newspapers from Massachusetts full of articles about the Boston Massacre and the Boston Tea Party, the ordinaries buzzed with talk.

When they weren't shouting about Parliament's Coercive Acts, townspeople and visiting farmers played darts and chess. They pitched horseshoes and played lively bowling games out on the village green. On the outskirts of the village, boys and young men raced horses while onlookers cheered. The blacksmith labored at his forge, the miller at his gristmill. Women visited with neighbors they hadn't seen for months. Chickens and pigs looked for scraps of food on the streets, while cows grazed on the village commons.

On Sundays, things were much quieter than during the rest of the week. The streets were empty and the ordinary was closed. In many of the colonies, there were laws requiring people to go to church. Everyone would put on their Sunday best to attend the long service.

The men donned waistcoats (vests), long coats, knee breeches, buckled shoes, and black three-cornered hats. In the bigger towns, the wealthiest

The Old Tun Tavern

gentlemen wore suits of silk and velvet, white silk stockings, ruffled collars and lace at their wrists, and satin vests embroidered with colorful flowers. Wealthy men wore wigs, though they were just beginning to go out of style. Some men powdered their hair and tied it back with a ribbon. (On windy days, the powder flew off behind them like a dust storm.) Their sons dressed like the men in miniature; some even wore wigs. Quakers and Puritans (two religious groups) dressed in simple black with no ruffles, wigs, or embroidery.

Women wore long gowns with sleeves, topped with a petticoat, then with a long skirt. Beneath their garments, stiff whalebone "stays" sewn into their bodices held in their waists (and cut off their breathing). Some wore bustles and hoops so wide they couldn't get through doors. Their dresses had sleeves with turned-back cuffs and frills. Wealthy women added long gloves and carried fans in the summer and muffs in the winter. Many wore masks of velvet or silk to protect their complexions from the sun and wind. They piled their hair up, added fake curls and ribbons, and kept it all in place with flour paste. They wore pattens (wooden clogs) or galoshes over their thin satin shoes to protect them from mud and dirt. Little girls dressed like their mothers, all the way down to tight stays and hoops. Country women wore plain linen dresses. They made their dresses last for years and wore their hair in a simple fashion, pinned up and covered with a cap. They tied kerchiefs around their shoulders and wore aprons over their dresses.

*The fashionable
Mrs. Alexander Hamilton*

Women spun and wove cloth to make clothes, blankets, and napkins. It would have been much easier to buy British cloth, but determined patriot women boycotting British goods made their cloth the hard way. There was so much spinning to do that women brought their spinning wheels

Homespun

If you wanted a new outfit in the 18th century, you had to plan ahead. Here's what it took to get a new linen dress or pair of breeches: Raise a crop of flax. Harvest. Remove the seeds (you can use them to make oil) and soak the stalks in water. Pound the stalks. Remove the bark and comb the remaining fibers over and over (and over!) again. Pound until soft. Spin fibers into thread on a spinning wheel. Bleach the thread, wash, rinse, and beat. Dry thread and wind onto bobbins. Weave thread into fabric on a loom. Measure for clothes, cut fabric, and sew new dress or breeches.

If you preferred wool, you raised a herd of sheep, sheared them, and dyed the wool with indigo (blue) or other colors made from bark, nuts, or flowers. Then the wool was combed, spun, and woven.

✦

with them when visiting friends so they could talk and work at the same time. Nothing went to waste; leftover pieces of fabric were used to make quilts. Frugal Martha Washington unraveled and rewove her old dresses and George's stockings into chair covers and pillowcases.

Many homes had a room on the main floor just for the spinning wheel and hand loom. The typical house had two rooms downstairs and two upstairs. The walls were whitewashed and the windows small (glass was very expensive). Upstairs rooms were shared by the brothers and sisters of large families. Furnishings were plain and made of wood. Bed frames held mattresses made of feathers or straw or cornhusks. There were no indoor bathrooms. In the cold winter and wet early spring, it seemed an awfully long way to the outhouse (called the "House of Necessity").

The warmest room in the house was the kitchen. In many homes, the parents slept there and tied their bed up against the wall during the day. Here a big iron pot hung over the fire and strings of drying apples, peppers, and squash hung overhead. A long wooden table was flanked by high-backed benches. Once a week, the children lined up in the kitchen to bathe in a washtub.

Southern families sat down to tables loaded with smoked ham, game meats, biscuits, and rice. New Englanders enjoyed clams, fish, and lobster. People north and south drank milk, cider, and ale (but rarely water). A visitor at John Adams's home wrote that he was served a hearty meal of veal, bacon, and neck of mutton with vegetables and cornbread—molasses and butter on the side.

In a more modest home, he might have tied a napkin around his neck and shared a one-pot meal of hash, stew, or porridge with the family. Everywhere, because there was no refrigeration, food was served fresh, smoked, salted, or dried. Northerners kept food cool with blocks of ice they'd cut from lakes in the wintertime. Southern colonists built stone springhouses over cool, running springwater. Here, they stored milk and other dairy products.

Women baked brown bread in hearth ovens while beans and stews simmered in iron pots over the fire. One child was given the job of turning the roast meat on its spit. Children also helped to churn butter and make cheese. In the summer and fall, families ate fresh greens from their gardens. They dug pits to store potatoes, turnips, and carrots for the winter. They picked apples and peaches from their orchards to make cider, pies, jams, and dried fruit. Late in the fall, they slaughtered hogs, hung the hams in the smokehouses, and made sausage and lard. They tapped maple trees for syrup and gathered honey from beehives.

In the winter, there were fewer chores to do. The men repaired their tools, traps, and nets. Boys and girls whittled wooden toys and made dolls (called "babies") of cornhusks. Bundled up against winter's cold, children skated on frozen ponds, held giant snowball fights, and went sledding down hills.

In the summer, children played many games still played today, including hide-and-seek, tag, blindman's buff, and "Scotch-hoppers" (hop-

Three Colonial Children's Games

For each of these games, the more kids, the better.

SKIN THE SNAKE

Stand in a line, one behind the other, with legs spread apart. Each child should reach between his or her legs with the left hand to grasp the right hand of the person behind. After doing this, the last person in the line lies down. Everyone else backs up over him or her without breaking the chain of hands. As each person reaches the end, he or she should lie down and let the line continue moving.

STOOL BALL

One player, holding a sturdy stick, sits on a three-legged stool. The other players stand at least 10 feet away and take turns throwing a soccer-sized ball at the stool, trying to knock it over. The person sitting on the stool can use the stick to knock the ball away. The person who knocks the stool over sits on it for the next turn.

I SENT A LETTER TO MY LOVE

Sit in a circle and sing this song while passing a letter around: "I sent a letter to my love and on the way I dropped it. One of you has picked it up and put it in your pocket. Please, please, drop it, drop it. Please, please, drop it, drop it." Whoever is holding the letter when the song ends has to stand up and run around the circle. The person who was sitting to this person's right stands up and chases the person holding the letter. The person with the letter tries to get back to his or her spot and sit down without being caught. If he or she makes it back to the spot, both sit down in their original places. If caught, he or she must sit behind the person who was chasing. Send the letter around and sing the song again. The winner is the last person left in the circle.

scotch). They spun tops, jumped rope, rolled hoops, and shot marbles. Checkers was popular, as were games such as Fox and Geese, King Am I, Chuck-farthing, and Tipcat. Town children gathered in the streets to watch acrobats and puppet shows. They and their parents enjoyed musical concerts, dances, and plays put on by traveling troupes of actors.

Many people kept diaries in which they described daily events and wrote out sayings and poems they wanted to remember. They read favorite books, such as *Robinson Crusoe* and

Boston Brown Bread and Churned Butter

Try serving this all-American bread with your own churned butter!

BREAD
(Makes 1 loaf)

What you need
1 loaf pan, 4 by 8 inches
Butter and flour for pan
½ cup rye flour
½ cup cornmeal
1 cup all-purpose white flour
½ teaspoon baking soda
1 teaspoon baking powder
½ teaspoon salt
2 mixing bowls
Wooden spoon
1 cup buttermilk
3 tablespoons melted butter
⅓ cup molasses
2 eggs
Oven mitts
Cooling rack

Preheat the oven to 350°F. Butter the loaf pan, then dust it lightly with flour. Combine the rye flour, cornmeal, white flour, baking soda, baking powder, and salt together in a mixing bowl. Stir the buttermilk, melted butter, molasses, and eggs together in another bowl. Pour the buttermilk mixture into the flour mixture and stir until combined. Pour into loaf pan and bake for 45 minutes. Remove from the oven with oven mitts and place on a rack to cool for 15 minutes. When cool, shake the bread gently out of the pan.

BUTTER
(Makes about 1 cup)

What you need
½ pint whipping cream
Large, wide-mouthed glass jar with tight-
    fitting lid
Colander

Pour the whipping cream into the jar and screw the lid on tight. Shake the jar vigorously back and forth. In 5 to 10 minutes, the mixture will start to look like whipped cream. Keep shaking. In a few more minutes, the cream will thicken into butter and a watery liquid will separate out. Pour the butter into a colander to strain out the liquid. Spread your hand-churned butter on a slice of Boston Brown Bread.

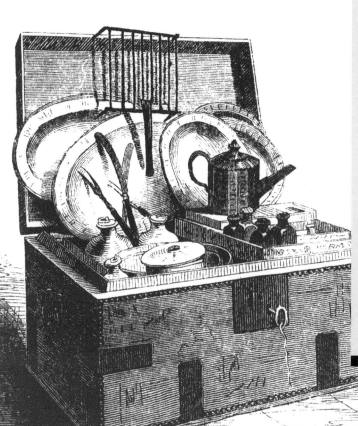

Papyrotamia

The art of creating decorative paper cutouts, called "papyrotamia," was a favorite pastime of the colonists. They made and framed detailed cutouts of flowers, landscapes, and curlicue patterns. You can make simple or elaborate paper art, from dolls to snowflakes to special designs. Mount them on cards to send to friends.

What you need
Paper (pick out different colors and
  weights)
Pencil
Scissors (you might want to have a small
  pair for delicate work)
Heavy paper or card stock for mounting
White glue

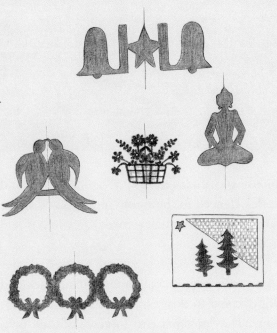

Choose paper. Fold it in half and draw the design on it. You might try some of the samples shown or make up your own. You could draw hearts and cupids for Valentine's Day, Christmas trees, flowers, castles, wreaths, or baskets of flowers.

Carefully trim the paper to cut out the design. You might find it easier to move the paper rather than the scissors as you cut. Use white glue to mount the paper design onto the heavy paper or card stock.

Gulliver's Travels, aloud to each other by the fire. The musically inclined played the harpsichord, flute, or violin. Young women embroidered samplers of pictures, alphabets, and verses. It was very popular to make paper silhouettes (profiles) and elaborate paper cutouts.

From the Frontier to Philadelphia

Life on the frontier was especially challenging. Though King George had set the colonies' boundary at the Appalachian Mountains, pioneers pushed farther west. Daniel Boone explored the wilderness beyond the mountains, then led a group of settlers over the Cumberland Gap to begin a community in Kentucky. When pioneer families came to their new home, they chopped down trees and built rough one-room, windowless cabins. As soon as they could, they cleared land and planted corn. Hunters dressed in fringed deerskin, with powder horns to carry their gunpowder hanging from their belts, carried their flintlock rifles into the forests to hunt deer, wild turkeys, and rabbits. Women cooked the game in iron pots and served it with cornbread.

At night, they bolted their doors against Indian attack. The native people who had lived so long in this land—among them the Shawnee, Delaware, Creek, and Cherokee tribes—were

sometimes threatened by the new settlers and waged war against them. Even Boone's family wasn't safe. Shawnee warriors kidnapped his daughter; two years later Boone was taken captive. (He was adopted into their tribe and later escaped to rejoin his settlement.)

In the southernmost colonies, there were few towns and the distances between neighbors were great. People were always eager for company and news. The owners of the large southern plantations sent their slaves out at night to hold lanterns along the dark roads and invite passing travelers to stop and stay.

Though there were slaves throughout the colonies, most worked on southern plantations, planting and harvesting tobacco, rice, and indigo crops. They worked from sunup to sundown tending to their masters' crops and livestock. When the masters' work was done, they tended to their own vegetable patches and set traps for animals. Late at night, slave families spent time together in their one-room cabins. They told stories, danced to the music of banjo and fiddle players, and prayed that someday freedom would be theirs.

Slavery had been practiced in the colonies from the earliest years. Some people, black and white, came to the colonies as indentured servants. They pledged 4 to 10 years of their lives in exchange for ship passage to America, food, clothing, and shelter. For the span of their contract, they were considered property. Africans were taken by force from their homelands and found themselves toiling for others in new lands as carpenters, blacksmiths, farmhands, and personal servants. By the late 1700s, more than 450,000 black slaves labored on farms, on plantations, and in towns throughout the colonies. They were property and could be bought and sold at their masters' will. Parents and children, husbands and wives were often separated at the auction block. Sometimes their masters beat

✦ Benjamin Franklin ✦
(1706–1790)

One of 17 children in a Boston family, Benjamin started working when he was 10. At 17, he went to Philadelphia with three cents in his pocket (he bought three loaves of bread and gave two of them away). A few years later, after a visit to London, he was an established publisher and businessman. He retired early from that career to pursue his passion for science.

Franklin served the colonies as postmaster, as delegate at the Second Continental Congress, and as the colonies' representative in France. After the war he helped create the new United States government at the Constitutional Convention. With his wife, Deborah, he raised three children (his son William grew up to be a loyalist and King George's royal governor of New Jersey).

Ben Franklin began every day with the question, "What good shall I do this day?" Perhaps that's why he accomplished so much. Franklin was a printer and publisher, inventor, scientist, philosopher, and statesman. He invented bifocals, the lightning rod, a type of odometer, and the Franklin Stove. He founded the first American circulating library. He figured out that lightning and electricity were related (by flying a kite with a metal key attached to it during a storm—don't try this yourself!). He taught himself four languages. He played the guitar, harp, and violin and invented a musical instrument called the "armonica." All this and more, yet he'd only gone to school for two years!

Benjamin Franklin at the Court of France

them. If they were caught running away, they were whipped.

Many blacks living in the colonies at this time were free. They worked off their indentured servitude with years of labor or were freed when their masters died. Some escaped to communities where no one knew them and made a new life with forged papers. Crispus Attucks, who was killed in the Boston Massacre, had escaped from slavery. He'd taught himself to read and write and became a sailor on a whaling ship.

A southern plantation was like a miniature town. Everything was made on the plantation, from bricks to bonnets. The owner's "big house" stood among slave quarters, stables, barns, smokehouses, icehouses, dairies, and shops for the blacksmith and carpenter. The cook prepared meals in a special kitchen separate from the house to keep the kitchen's heat away from the living quarters.

Boston, New York, and Charleston, South Carolina, were big towns, but the largest and finest town in the colonies was Philadelphia. Its busy wharves were lined with ships carrying goods to and from England. Its tree-lined cobblestone streets were crowded with wagons and carriages. Craftsmen and artisans lived and worked in busy shops alongside the brick homes of the town's residents. Tailors and hatters, innkeepers and booksellers kept up busy trades.

Philadelphia had modern conveniences such as water pumps for its citizens. At night, its streets were brightly lit with whale oil lamps. Night watchmen patrolled the streets looking out for

ACTIVITY

Assemble an Almanac

Almanacs include important dates, weather forecasts, and practical tips. Franklin pretended his almanac was the creation of "Poor Richard," a country printer with a lot to say. You may have heard some of his wise and witty epigrams (short sayings) such as "haste makes waste," "never leave till tomorrow what you can do today," and even "no pain, no gain." (Though he really said, "There are no gains without pains.")

Make your own almanac. Fill it with important dates in history, holidays (real and made up), predictions, fun facts, advice, jokes, drawings, and your own epigrams. Make it for next year and give it away as a Christmas present. Or pretend you're Ben Franklin living in the 1700s. What kind of news and advice would you print for your fellow colonists? You might share home remedies, predict troubles with the mother country, or celebrate King George's birthday (June 4).

What you need

3 to 6 sheets of paper, 8½ inches by 11 inches (3 sheets will make 12 pages; 6 sheets will make 24)

Scissors

Pens, pencils, ruler, paints, and paintbrushes

2 pieces of colored cardboard, each cut to 6 inches by 9 inches

Hole puncher

Ribbon or long, colored pipe cleaner

Fold the sheets of paper in half lengthwise. Press along the crease, then unfold. Cut along the crease. Fill the pages with your own wit and wisdom. Decorate the two pieces of cardboard, which will be your front and back covers.

Place the pages between the two pieces of cardboard so that all the paper and cardboard line up on the left and the papers are centered between the top and bottom of the cardboard pieces. Hold tightly with one hand so the pages don't slip, and with your other hand punch 6 holes along the left edge. Bind the booklet with ribbon or colored pipe cleaner.

fires. Every hour they called out the time and weather.

The fire watch was Ben Franklin's idea. Franklin was Philadelphia's busiest man. He helped organize the fire department, an orphanage, a hospital, a militia, the night watch, a college (today's University of Pennsylvania), and published the city newspaper, too. Nearly every household had a copy of his *Poor Richard's Almanac*. For 25 years, Franklin published this almanac under the pen name of Richard Saunders.

Long before the troubles with England, Franklin had proposed that the colonies unite for protection and self-government. In 1754, he printed a woodcut in his newspaper that showed a snake divided into pieces, each piece representing a colony, and a caption reading "Join or Die." Now, many colonists agreed with him. People from distant towns and villages sent goods to Boston to support the patriots whose port was closed by British troops. Rice was brought north from the Carolinas, bread from Maryland, and a big flock of sheep from the people of Connecticut.

The colonists had flourished in their new home because they were hard-working and independent. Communities thrived because neighbors depended on each other. They worked together to clear land, raise barns, and harvest crops. Now, facing this new crisis, the people from different backgrounds across the colonies had to learn to join together, or they would fall apart.

JOIN or DIE

three

"We Must All Hang Together"

Fall, 1774: A Meeting in Philadelphia

Patrick Henry summed up the new feeling in the colonies. "The distinctions between Virginians, Pennsylvanians, New Yorkers, and New Englanders are no more," he declared. "I am not a Virginian, but an American!" The delegates at the First Continental Congress murmured their agreement. These 56 men, representing all the colonies except Georgia, had made their way on horseback and in coaches to Philadelphia. George Washington, Thomas Jefferson, and Patrick Henry were among the delegates from Virginia. Samuel Adams's neighbors had presented him with a new suit of clothes so he could represent them in style. John Adams brought his diary to write about his experiences.

Crossing the Delaware

The delegates called themselves the "Continental Congress." They met at Philadelphia's State House (today called "Independence Hall"). They chose a leader to run the meeting (Peyton Randolph, a cousin of Jefferson's) and gave him the title of "president." They agreed that each colony would have an equal vote on their decisions, no matter how large or small its population, and they set to work planning a response to the Coercive Acts. Great Britain, in trying to crush the uprising in Massachusetts, had caused all of the colonies to join together. "It was like thirteen clocks striking as one," said John Adams.

Though the delegates meant business, most didn't intend to break away entirely from their mother country. Their hope was for a say in their government. They talked and talked (for everyone had a different opinion) about the best way to reach their goal, then agreed on the "Suffolk

Patrick Henry
(1736–1799)

Patrick Henry had a way with words. Many of his rang out during the years of the American Revolution when he was a lawyer, a member of Virginia's House of Burgesses, and a Continental Congress delegate. Some people said Henry's speeches made their hair stand on end and their blood run cold. He gave one of his most famous speeches right before the war. "We have done everything that could be done to avert the storm!" he exclaimed. "Is life so dear or peace so sweet as to be purchased at the price of chains and slavery? I know not what course others may take but as for me, give me liberty or give me death!"

Resolves." This document was written by Dr. Joseph Warren in Massachusetts and brought to Philadelphia—at a gallop—by Paul Revere. It rejected the Coercive Acts and the Quebec Act. It urged the people in the colonies to collect their own taxes and ban all trade with Great Britain until things got straightened out. And though they didn't want war, the members of the Congress thought the colonists should arm themselves. With the British holding Boston under military rule, who knew what would happen next? They passed a resolution that the colonies should form militias (groups of citizen-soldiers).

Next, the Congress sent a petition to King George and the people of Great Britain demanding that, as loyal subjects, they be granted the same rights as Englishmen. Then they adjourned, agreeing to gather the next spring if necessary. By the time they met again, the first shots of a long war had been fired.

April 19, 1775:
"The Shot Heard
'Round the World"

Back in Boston, British general Thomas Gage prepared for the worst. His spies warned him that the colonists were stashing arms, gunpowder, and shot. It was no secret that men were drilling in villages throughout Massachusetts. When these men heard their signal (a drumbeat or church bell), they left their plows and forges, grabbed their weapons, and ran to their assigned meeting place. Because they trained to be ready for action at a moment's notice, they were called "minutemen." When Gage heard about all this activity, he ordered his soldiers to fortify the outskirts of Boston and sent to London for more troops. "If you think ten thousand men sufficient, send twenty," he wrote.

When King George heard that the colonists were arming themselves, he felt betrayed. Parliament declared Massachusetts to be in a state of rebellion and ordered General Gage to bring the disloyal colony to its knees.

Gage learned that the colonists had stockpiled a large store of military supplies in Concord (about 20 miles from Boston). He readied his soldiers to march there to destroy the arms, gunpowder, candles, and medicines. Concord was also the meeting place of the rebellious leaders of Massachusetts. Gage had special orders to arrest the biggest troublemakers, Samuel Adams and John Hancock.

Seven hundred British troops left Boston on this mission. Under the cover of darkest night, with oars muffled, they paddled across the town's Charles River. But their mission was no secret—the patriots had learned about General Gage's plan. (Some say they found out from the general's American wife!) By a prearranged signal, silversmith and patriot Paul Revere let watchful friends know about the British troop movement. Two lanterns hung from a church steeple told friends across the river that the British were com-

The die is now cast, the Colonies must either submit or triumph.

—KING GEORGE III

ing by sea. If the soldiers had marched out of Boston by land, one lantern would have been hung. Then Revere set out on horseback to nearby Lexington, where Adams and Hancock were staying, to warn them. He shouted the news of the British march to people in villages along the way.

The red-coated soldiers marched in step through the night. As the sun rose, they were near Lexington. Here the advance troops were faced with minutemen—teenagers and grandfathers, fathers and sons—lined up along the village green. "Disperse, ye Rebels! Lay down your arms and

★   ACTIVITY   ★

Get Ready in a Minute

In one short minute, the Massachusetts minutemen dropped everything and gathered at the village commons. Can you get ready in a minute?

What you need

2 or more friends

Minuteman clothes and equipment (see Chapters 3 and 6 for instructions on making a three-cornered hat, a fringed hunting shirt, and a powder horn and pouch; use a stick as a pretend rifle)

A bell or whistle

Stopwatch or watch with second hand

Pick an outside meeting place where you will all gather after hearing the signal. Choose one person to be a timekeeper. Lay your minuteman clothes and equipment out in your room, ready to go. Then go outside and pretend it's the 18th century. Pretend to plow, feed the animals, or chop wood.

The British are coming! The timekeeper blows the whistle or rings the bell and starts keeping time with the watch. The race begins! Run to your room, change your clothes, and pick up your equipment. Run out to the assigned meeting place. Did you make it in a minute? The timekeeper salutes the first person to arrive, and then lets him or her take over as timekeeper. Play until everyone makes it in a minute.

Midnight Riders

Listen my children, and you shall hear
Of the midnight ride of ... William Dawes?

A poem by Henry Wadsworth Longfellow tells of the famous ride of Paul Revere. Revere rode many times and many miles as an express rider for the patriots, but on this night he was not the only rider. William Dawes, Dr. Samuel Prescott, and others also galloped through villages to spread the word. Church bells rang and drummers beat signals. Women reached for their children and minutemen for their muskets. In Lexington, Revere found the home where Adams and Hancock were sleeping. A guard at the door hushed him, saying he was making too much noise. "Noise!" Revere replied, "You'll have noise enough before long!" He shouted to Adams and Hancock that they were in danger. The two escaped before the redcoats arrived.

Dawes, Prescott, and Revere left Lexington together and galloped furiously for Concord. They were ambushed by patrolling British officers. Dawes and Prescott escaped; Dr. Prescott made it to Concord to warn the villagers. When the British officers learned that the countryside was alarmed and preparing for attack, they let Revere go and raced for their units.

Paul Revere's Ride

Battle of Lexington

disperse!" shouted British major John Pitcairn. The Americans, greatly outnumbered, began to break rank and walk away, though few laid down their arms. At that moment, a shot went off. No one knows who fired it; it may have been an accident. But when the British soldiers heard it, they began firing at will. Eight Americans were killed.

The British troops marched on to Concord to search for the stashed arms and military supplies. The villagers, forewarned, hid many of the supplies. What the redcoats found, they burned. After a brief and sharp scuffle with gathering minutemen and militia, the British troops fell back and began a withdrawal to Boston.

By that time, news of the events at Lexington had spread throughout the countryside. As the British troops marched, men from nearby villages shot at them from behind trees and rocks. The exhausted British soldiers were very relieved when reinforcements arrived from Boston. With this help, they retreated to safety. The first shots had been fired; war had begun.

Over the next days, Dr. Warren treated the American wounded and organized the volunteers who showed up to fight for the patriot cause. Soon more than 10,000 gathered outside Boston, ready and eager to fight. Artemus Ward, who had fought in the French and Indian War, took command of this ragtag army. He set them to work digging fortifications and standing guard.

General Gage kept his 5,000 British soldiers inside Boston. Help was on the way. King George was sending warships, troops, and three generals—John Burgoyne, Henry Clinton, and William Howe—to America. One of the generals, Sir Henry Clinton, had grown up in the colonies. His father had been royal governor of New York. Sir William Howe had fought alongside colonists in the French and Indian War. As a member of Parliament, he had sworn that he would never carry arms against the colonists; now he had to take back that promise. John Burgoyne was a great favorite among the British soldiers, who called him "Gentleman Johnny." He was a successful playwright and quite a dandy. When he heard that British soldiers in Boston were surrounded by angry Americans, John Burgoyne said, "The King's troops shut up? Well, let us get in and we'll soon find elbow room!"

The Americans had fighting spirit but not much in the way of supplies. The volunteers brought muskets, if they had them, or showed up armed with sickles and scythes (both curved metal blades). One of their leaders, Benedict Arnold, knew they would never be able to stand up to the British without cannons. He offered to lead an expedition against British-held Forts Ticonderoga and Crown Point on Lake Champlain. He thought he could easily capture the forts and their big guns.

Arnold set off to find that someone else had the same good idea. Ethan Allen, the leader of a rough and ready group called the "Green Mountain Boys," was also planning an attack against Fort Ticonderoga. Together, they led the Green Mountain Boys in a surprise attack. Giant Ethan Allen waved his sword and, with a roar, demanded surrender "in the name of the Great Jehovah and the Continental Congress!" The surprised commander surrendered the fort, along with its precious guns, boats, and supplies.

On the same day that Fort Ticonderoga fell, the Continental Congress gathered in Philadelphia. So much had changed since their last meeting. Some delegates still hoped for peace under Britain's rule. Others wanted to break from their mother country. Benjamin Franklin called for liberty. George Washington showed up in the blue and white military uniform he'd worn in the French and Indian War. Philadelphians went wild with excitement when Samuel Adams and John Hancock arrived (Hancock loved the attention—he rode through town accompanied by clattering horsemen with their sabers drawn). Hancock was elected president of this Congress. John Adams was everywhere, convincing all the delegates that they should work together. He

Capture of Fort Ticonderoga

❖ George Washington ❖
(1732–1799)

Forget the wooden teeth and the cherry tree—they're both myths. But George Washington did have false teeth (several sets, of ivory and cow's teeth) and telling lies wasn't his style. George's father, a Virginia planter, died when he was a boy. As a teenager, George worked as a surveyor, then inherited his brother's estate, Mount Vernon. At 19, he was an officer in Virginia's militia. He fought side by side with the British in the French and Indian War, then came home to marry Martha Custis, a widow with two children. His hopes for a quiet life changed when he went to Philadelphia as a Continental Congress delegate and was elected commander of the new army.

Washington was tall (6 feet, 4 inches—at that time, a giant) and fair skinned. His face was marked with smallpox scars. He was athletic, loved to ride horses and hunt, and had spent years roughing it in the western wilds. According to Thomas Jefferson, he was the best dancer in Virginia. He was also shy, serious, generous, and brave and worked hard to control his hot temper. As a young man, Washington was determined to improve himself through reading and study. He copied down "Rules of Civility and Decent Behavior" and followed them unfailingly. (The rules ranged from the sensible to the silly, from "respect your elders," "listen when others speak," and "don't point or roll your eyes" to "cleanse not your teeth with the tablecloth but if others do so let it be done without a peep to them.") His soldiers adored him and so did the American people. When the war was over, they elected him as their first president.

Dance a Minuet

George Washington loved to dance, and his favorite dance was the minuet. There were many versions of the minuet, all of them elegant and graceful. Put on your finest clothes and your finest airs and dance like General Washington!

What you need
A partner

Start in the center of the dance floor with your partner and first acknowledge the audience. The gentleman bows from the waist and the lady curtsies. Then bow and curtsy to each other.

Turn with your partner toward one corner of the dance floor. Stand side by side, with the lady to the gentleman's right. The lady crooks her elbow and holds her left hand so that the palm faces the gentleman; he places his right hand on her raised left hand. Move toward the corner, taking small steps, starting with the right foot. Right, left, right, then point your left toe out and tap it on the floor three times. Now move forward again, this time starting with the left foot. Left, right, left, then point your right toe out and tap it on the floor three times. Continue until you reach the corner of the floor.

When you get near the corner, slowly lower the hands that were touching and, while turning toward each other, raise the opposite hands. By the time you are facing all the way around toward the opposite corner, the lady's right hand should be touching the gentleman's left. Begin dancing toward the other corner of the room. When you reach that corner, turn again and dance to the center of the room. Release hands, back slightly away from each other, and bow and curtsy.

Don't forget that the minuet is executed with the utmost grace and style. Every step should be dignified and elegant. Keep your back straight, your chin up, eyebrows raised, and only the slightest smile on your face.

proposed that the armed men outside Boston be recognized as America's "Continental Army" and that they be led by George Washington. Washington, when he heard his name, blushed and left the room. A unanimous vote made Washington commander in chief of the American army.

June 17, 1775:
The Battle of Bunker Hill

By the time Washington reached his army, they had already been in battle. Inside Boston, British general Gage had welcomed reinforcements and the three new generals from England. The Americans outside the town heard that the British planned to seize the high ground around their camp and destroy them. They decided to make their move before the redcoats had a chance. They moved to a hill across the river from Boston, overlooking the town of Charlestown. From this position on Breed's Hill (later renamed for nearby Bunker's Hill), they threatened British ships and troops in Boston. The British replied to this insolence with artillery fire from their ships, which set Charlestown on fire. General Gage ordered British general William Howe to send soldiers across the river and up the hill against the Americans.

This order was a terrible mistake on Gage's part. Though his troops were organized, brave, and well trained, they were no match for the Americans' position. The redcoats advanced uphill, carrying heavy packs and weapons, while the Americans waited behind bales of hay and earthen walls they'd built the night before. American commanders William Prescott and Israel Putnam ordered their men to hold their fire until the enemy was near—"close enough to see the whites of their eyes." They had very little ammunition and every shot would count.

For hours, the British troops tried to take the hill. Again and again, the redcoats marched up the slopes, only to fall when they came within range of American fire. They retreated, regathered, and attacked again until nearly half their number were killed or wounded. Beneath them, Charlestown's buildings burned and crashed to the ground. Cannons roared from the British ships, and army musicians tried to inspire the troops with fife and drum music. The townspeople of Boston gathered in every high place, from church steeples and rooftops to the masts of ships in the wharves, to watch the fight. Abigail Adams took her young son, John Quincy Adams, to the top of a hill and together they watched this first battle between British and American soldiers.

When the Americans ran out of ammunition, they retreated. The British won the heights but at a huge cost in lives. Because of the losses, General Gage was soon removed as top commander and General William Howe put in his place.

The American losses were not as great, but they mourned for one in particular. Dr. Joseph Warren had come to fight on the hill despite a premonition that he would meet his death there. He stayed to the end to help others retreat, then was killed by a musket ball.

George Washington was relieved to hear his men would stand and fight. But when he arrived and looked his army up and down, he knew he had a lot of work to do to make them into real soldiers. They were dressed in the clothes they

BOSTON

CHARLES TO

Attack on Bunker Hill and the Burning of Charlestown

wore from home and sleeping in makeshift tents of blankets and sailcloth. Some had muskets or hunting rifles, but their powder horns and ammunition pouches were nearly empty. Others had no weapons at all. Washington shuddered to think what would happen if the British knew about their predicament. It was a great day when a resourceful book peddler, Henry Knox, brought 59 cannons captured from Fort Ticonderoga to the Continental Army camp. Knox had brought the guns 300 miles down rivers and over snowy terrain. Washington made the book peddler his captain of artillery and, later, a general.

Putnam's Prank

Israel Putnam fought in the French and Indian War, was captured by Indians, and, as a white-haired old man, led the fight at Bunker Hill. Once, he'd been challenged to a duel by a British officer. Putnam was allowed to choose the weapons and picked two kegs of gunpowder. He and his opponent each sat on a keg while their long fuses were lit. As the fuses burned down, Putnam's challenger lost his nerve, jumped up, and ran away. Putnam sat on his keg and laughed. The kegs weren't really filled with gunpowder. His opponent had run away from a barrel of onions.

✤

Make a Tricorn Hat

The soldiers didn't have uniforms, but many of them wore black, three-cornered hats in the hottest 18th-century style. Top yourself off with a tricorn hat!

What you need
Long piece of paper
Tape
Chalk
18 by 18-inch square piece of heavy cardboard (recycle a box)
Ruler
Scissors
18 by 18-inch square piece of black felt
Pins
Needle
Black thread

Circle your head with the long piece of paper, just above your ears, and tape it (as shown).

Draw a dot with the chalk in the center of the heavy cardboard. Center the circle of paper around that dot and trace its outline onto the cardboard. Pretending the outline you traced is a clock, draw dots at 12:00, 4:00, and 8:00 on the outline. Using the ruler, draw a straight line from the dot in the center through the 12:00 dot to a point 3 inches beyond it. Do the same at 4:00 and 8:00. Connect the three outside dots to make a triangle. (See illustration.) Cut out the triangle. Cut out the circle in the center.

With the chalk, draw a circle 18 inches in diameter on the felt. Cut out the circle. Cover your head with the circle of felt. Place the triangular piece over it and push down until it fits snugly. Carefully pull it off your head, keeping the felt crown (top) of the hat stable. Pin the outside edge of the felt, in the middle of each side of the triangle, to the three sides of the crown.

With needle and thread, stitch the felt to the crown where you pinned it. Remove the pins. At each side of the triangle, flip the fabric over the cardboard and sew it to the crown.

The men didn't act like an army either; they wandered about as they pleased and left for home whenever they felt like it. They didn't much like taking orders. Some of them didn't like each other. Washington had to get off his horse and personally break up a snowball fight that turned into a big brawl between Virginia and Massachusetts soldiers. But in a short time, he organized the men into regiments and imposed rules and discipline. He set them to work gathering food and firewood, digging earthworks, and standing guard. If he could only keep them from leaving when their short enlistments were up, they might actually be able to stand up against the British.

1775–1776: Boston and Quebec Under Siege

After the Battle of Bunker Hill, Boston's patriots hastily fled the town. Loyalists (colonists loyal to the crown) moved into Boston to be under the protection of the British army. The redcoats drilled and prepared for the next battle. Every day, General Washington expected they would come out of the town and overrun his vulnerable army. If they knew, Washington fretted, that his Continental Army only had 32 barrels of powder, then the war would soon be lost.

While Washington's soldiers waited outside Boston, others made their way north. Two American forces marched to Canada on a secret mission, hoping to take the territory away from the British. Benedict Arnold led one of the forces north on a brutal march through uncharted forests in cruel weather. Hundreds of his men died from disease and starvation along the way. American Richard Montgomery successfully brought his force against Montreal, then joined Arnold to storm the stronghold of Quebec. After a long winter siege outside its gates, they threw themselves against Quebec in a surprise midnight attack. In the brutal hand-to-hand fighting, many were killed (including Montgomery) or taken prisoner.

British ships attacked places up and down the coast in an attempt to lure Washington away from Boston. They burned Falmouth (now Portland), Maine. They shelled Norfolk, Virginia, and burned it down. Washington's home at nearby Mount Vernon and his wife, Martha, were in danger; she left to join her husband at his army camp.

Farther south, North Carolina militiamen gathered to thwart loyalist forces organized by the royal governor. While some people chose to fight for the patriot cause, others sided with the king. Here, former Scottish Highlanders joined the British cause. Dressed in kilts and armed with broadswords, they were marching to Wilmington, North Carolina, to join British troops when the patriots ambushed them. While bagpipes played, the Highlanders charged, crying, "King George and the Broadswords!" Their swords were no match for patriot guns, and their march ended at Widow Moore's Creek. The patriot

The Coat Roll

Supplies were scarce in the Continental Army. Congress asked the women of the colonies to help. Patriotic women busied themselves at spinning wheels and looms to make warm woolen coats for the soldiers. Inside each coat, the women sewed their own names and that of their hometown. Each soldier who volunteered for an eight-month stint at this time received one of these coats of homespun wool. The list of these soldiers was known as the "Coat Roll." The coats were prized by men who would otherwise have suffered in the bitter cold, and they provided the English with a nickname for the Continental Army—the "Homespuns."

victory inspired North Carolinians to adopt the "Halifax Resolves," a demand for independence from Great Britain.

On the outskirts of Boston, Washington grew tired of waiting. He came up with a plan to drive the redcoats out of town. One dark night, he moved his men onto a hill and ordered them to quickly build fortifications. When General Howe scanned the horizon the next morning, he was shocked to see American guns pointing down at him. His attempts to drive Washington's men from the hill were foiled by a huge storm. By the time the storm passed and the British were ready to attack again, the Americans had built another fort, this one even closer. Howe sent up a white flag of truce. Within days, 12,000 British soldiers and thousands of their loyalist followers sailed out of Boston's harbor. Boston was freed. General Washington moved his army to New York, where he expected the British to attack next.

July 4, 1776:
The First Fourth

Congress tried one last time to make things right with England. Delegate John Dickinson drafted an "Olive Branch" Petition (the olive branch is an emblem of peace) and sent it to King George. The king felt that the colonies were declaring war and trying to make peace at the same time. He wouldn't even read the petition. The next document they sent got his attention.

Virginia delegate Richard Henry Lee stood up in Congress one day and proposed that the connection between the colonies and Great Britain be dissolved. Thomas Jefferson was chosen to write the document that declared the colonies free from Great Britain's rule. (Jefferson thought Adams should write it. Adams declined. "I'm unpopular," he said, "and you write ten times better than me.") After many late nights in his rented room, Jefferson finished his "Declaration of Independence." It outlined the grievances against King George and stated that the "United Colonies are and ought to be free and independent States."

In words that changed the path of history, Jefferson stated the noble principles that "all men are created equal, that they are endowed by their Creator with certain unalienable Rights, that among these are Life, Liberty, and the pursuit of Happiness." The role of government was to secure these rights, Jefferson stated. Since Great Britain was not doing so, the American people were claiming their right to break away. With this Declaration, the rebellion of the colonies changed from an argument about taxes to a first step toward creating a new kind of government, one based on principles of equality and human rights.

On the 4th of July, 1776, the delegates gathered to sign Jefferson's document. John Hancock was the first to put his quill to the parchment. He signed with a flourish, large enough "for King

Reading of the Declaration of Independence

Signing the Declaration of Independence

✤ Thomas Jefferson ✤

(1743–1826)

Tall and bony, red-haired, shy among strangers and lively with friends, Thomas Jefferson was the eldest son of a Virginia planter and surveyor. He liked to swim, play violin, and ride horses, but most of all he was driven to learn. Jefferson studied 15 hours a day! In the mornings, he studied science, religion, and law. Every afternoon, he read about politics and history. He saved evenings for languages and literature.

At the time of the Declaration of Independence, Jefferson was 32 years old and one of the youngest delegates. He had been a lawyer and member of Virginia's House of Burgesses and had married a young widow named Martha. He would later become minister to France, George Washington's secretary of state, and the third president of the United States. Jefferson was also an architect, gardener, inventor, musician, naturalist, surveyor, and founder of the University of Virginia. (All that studying paid off!)

George to read without spectacles." Hancock turned to Benjamin Franklin and said, "We must be unanimous. There must be no pulling different ways. We must all hang together." Franklin knew that signing the document was treason and could mean death for all the signers, but he could never resist making a joke. "Yes," he agreed. "We must indeed all hang together or most assuredly we shall all hang separately."

Carrying copies of the radical document, couriers rode furiously to towns across the land. They posted the Declaration on liberty trees and read it aloud on street corners. In Philadelphia, the State House bell (now called the "Liberty Bell") rang loudly. In New York, General Washington read the Declaration to his soldiers. John Adams, in a letter to his wife, Abigail, predicted that America's independence would be celebrated for generations to come with parades and "illuminations" (fireworks). That year, Americans across the land celebrated with bells and bonfires.

Well, I Declare!

Printer John Dunlap made around 200 copies of the Declaration of Independence. Only 25 still exist. One was recently discovered in a four-dollar frame purchased at a flea market. It sold at auction for $8.1 million!

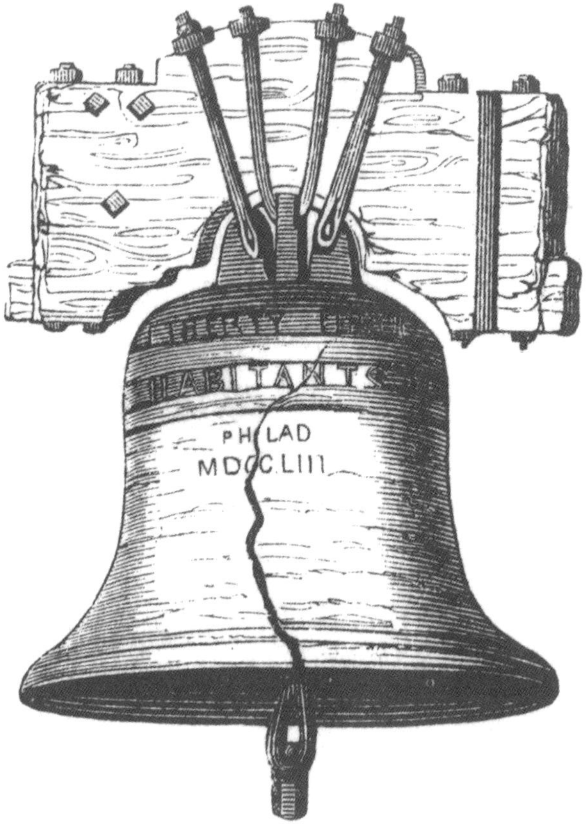

Even as Jefferson wrote the Declaration of Independence, a fleet of British ships under Admiral Sir Peter Parker sailed toward Charleston, South Carolina. Colonel William Moultrie and his patriot forces got ready for them. They melted down church windows to make lead for their musket balls and built a fort of logs and dirt on Sullivans Island. They withstood a nine-hour bombardment and repelled the British fleet.

The Liberty Bell

Shortly after it arrived from London in 1752, the Philadelphia State House bell developed a crack. Was it an omen of future relations between England and its colonies? Foundrymen recast it. More than 20 years later, on July 8, 1776, its ring drew people to the first reading of the Declaration of Independence. It cracked again on another July 8, in 1835, while ringing for the funeral of John Marshall, chief justice of the Supreme Court.

Battle of Long Island

August 27, 1776: The Battle of Long Island

In New York, shocked patriots watched as hundreds of British ships approached their town. There were so many, one onlooker wrote, that their masts looked like a forest of bare trees. Two of the ships sailed up the Hudson River and fired their guns. As cannonballs fell in the streets, families ran from their homes.

The fleet of ships carried 30,000 experienced and professional soldiers. Eight thousand were German soldiers who had been "rented" to the British king for seven pounds each. Because many of these soldiers came from a region called Hesse-Cassell, the Americans called them all "Hessians." Ten thousand sailors were under the command of Admiral Lord Richard Howe (brother to British commander in chief General Sir William Howe). The Continental Army, a mix of youngsters, old men, backwoodsmen, and inexperienced townsmen, was outnumbered almost two to one.

The mismatched forces met on Long Island. The Americans built fortifications on high ground but British general Sir Henry Clinton spotted the weak point in their lines. He moved some men to this unguarded side and other men behind and in front of the Americans. The British attacked from three directions, and the Americans collapsed. Those who could escape ran in the one direction left open—marshy ground that slowed their every desperate step. That night, as they huddled around their small campfires, the bright promise of independence seemed dim. They were cornered, with their backs to the East River, and would surely be captured.

Their general was not one to give up so easily. Late that night, when a helpful fog rolled in, Washington ordered his men to gather in absolute silence. He placed them, with all their baggage and artillery, aboard small boats and ferried them across the river to Manhattan. They left their fires lit so watching British sentries (guards) would think they were still in camp. When the British broke into the camp at daybreak, the last boat, carrying Washington, was just pulling away.

Washington stationed his men at different points around Manhattan Island but knew it would be impossible to hold it. His army was badly outnumbered, and, with Manhattan surrounded by water, the British could land anywhere.

His worst fears came true when British and Hessian troops landed on Manhattan's east side. Washington rode forward to see his panicked men dropping their muskets and packs and racing away. He planted his horse across their path and lashed out with his riding whip, but the men couldn't be stopped. As the redcoats marched forward, Washington sat on his horse and scowled at them, too, angry enough to attack by himself. Finally, his aide came forward and pulled Washington's horse away. When his men were safely north of town at Harlem Heights, Washington looked them over and wondered how these

Famous Last Words

American captain Nathan Hale was a schoolmaster posing as a spy for General Washington. One day he was captured by the British and allowed one last chance to speak before he was hung. "I only regret," said Nathan Hale, "that I have but one life to lose for my country."

❧

troops could possibly win a war against the finest army in the world.

The following day, in the Battle of Harlem Heights, Washington's soldiers showed more courage and gave as good as they got. Still, the British held Manhattan and continued on the attack. Day after day, the Americans fell back. A sharp fight at White Plains raised hopes, but when the British captured Forts Washington and Lee on the Hudson River, Washington lost heart. Three thousand of his men were taken prisoner and precious supplies seized.

With the enemy close on their heels, Washington led his discouraged troops across New Jersey. As they approached the Delaware River, British general Cornwallis's troops closed in behind them. Quickly, the Americans seized every boat for 75 miles up and down the river, paddled across the Delaware, and left the British standing on the opposite shore. Cornwallis had no way to follow. He stationed Hessian troops along the Delaware River and returned to British headquarters in New York.

With winter's onset, the British retired from battle. In those days, armies rarely fought in the wintertime. It was hard to get food for the men and fodder for the horses and cattle. Rain and snow turned roads to mud, and no one could march anywhere.

Winter—and Benedict Arnold—stopped a British invasion from Canada that year. When British forces sailed down Lake Champlain to retake Fort Ticonderoga, patriots under Arnold's command met them in hastily made galleys (large

rowboats). Their battle lasted for days. The men labored at their long oars, maneuvering the boats into position. Crashing volleys of gunfire crossed the waters. Though the British fleet gained the victory, it was useless to them. It was too late in the year to advance any farther. The British returned north to settle in for the winter, leaving Lake Champlain and Fort Ticonderoga to the Americans.

In Washington's camp, things looked very bleak. The British held Manhattan and New Jersey and were threatening Pennsylvania. The Continental Army was reduced to only 3,000 men. Thousands had been taken prisoner (including Washington's most senior general, Charles Lee—captured in his nightshirt while drinking his morning coffee). Others had fallen in battle. Some went home when their enlistments were up. Still more would leave on December 31 when their one-year period of enlistment ended. How could Washington convince them to stay when things seemed so hopeless?

Christmastime, 1776: The Battles of Trenton and Princeton

"The game is pretty near up," Washington wrote to his brother. Yet he couldn't bring himself to surrender all hope. His army built a makeshift camp in the winter chill. Soldiers from scattered

They cannot conquer an idea with an army.

—Thomas Paine

units trickled in. The general knew he was about to lose this army. They had fought and lost and were ready to go home when their enlistments expired at year's end. Washington had to do something now or all would be lost.

On Christmas, Washington took his chance. He marched his men, under cover of night, to the Delaware River to make a dangerous crossing. The soldiers poled their boats across the swift river in a blizzard of sleet and snow. They fought against the bitter wind and strained their eyes looking for ice floes that could capsize their small boats. After four perilous hours, Washington had a small army of men, horses, and cannons across the Delaware River. They made ready to attack the Hessians who were quartered at Trenton, eight miles away. The risk was great. If the attack failed, Washington's small force would be trapped, their backs to the river.

The men marched in darkness across the ice and snow. Many had no shoes and had wrapped their feet in rags. These left bloody footprints in the snow as they marched. They were freezing and tired and the weather was getting worse by the hour. Their general rode up and down their lines to encourage them. When they saw him in the torchlight and heard his quiet, "Press on, boys," they took heart.

Thomas Paine

In Trenton, the Hessians weren't thinking much about fighting. The Americans were weak, and no one fought in the wintertime anyway. The Hessian colonel carelessly posted few pickets (soldiers assigned to guard the camp) while

Common Sense

"These are the times that try men's souls. The summer soldier and the sunshine patriot will, in this crisis, shrink from the service of their country, but...he whose heart is firm...will pursue his principles unto death."

Patriot Thomas Paine wrote these words in the flickering light of a campfire, using a drumhead for a desk. He was the author of *Common Sense*, a 50-page pamphlet that roused the colonists to revolt. "We have in our power to begin the world anew," he wrote. This book "is working a powerful change in the minds of many men," said George Washington to a friend. Many who were not sure they wanted to rebel against Great Britain changed their minds after reading *Common Sense*.

❖

Washington at Princeton

he and his men celebrated Christmas. That evening, a loyalist citizen came to warn him that Washington was on the march. The colonel refused to admit the stranger. The loyalist scribbled a warning on a note, but when it was delivered, the colonel put it in his pocket unread.

Their footsteps silenced by new-fallen snow, the Americans were able to catch the Hessians completely off guard. The surprised Hessians spilled out of houses to turn their cannons against the Americans but were quickly overrun. They threw down their guns and flags. In the surprise attack, the Americans captured 1,000 prisoners and their much-needed arms.

A few days later, though the snow had deepened and the ice was even thicker, the Americans once more crossed the Delaware River.

British general Cornwallis had been about to go to England for the winter when he heard about Washington's surprise attack. He gathered his troops and prepared for a fight.

It was the 30th of December, and many American soldiers had reached the end of their enlistment period. Washington stood before them and made his plea. "You have worn yourselves out with fatigues and hardships but we know not how to spare you," he told them. He offered each a 10-dollar bounty from his own pocket. He convinced many to stay. They fought valiantly against Cornwallis's men near Trenton, then, in a surprise move, slipped around Cornwallis to capture British stores and their guard at Princeton. Despair began to turn to hope. Perhaps all was not yet lost.

John Burgoyne

Battle of Bennington

four

An Eventful Year

Summer, 1777: The Three-Pronged Plan

The year-end victories gave the Continental Army new heart. From their winter camp in Morristown, New Jersey, they raided and struck, keeping the British wary and on edge. By spring, new and eager volunteers swelled their ranks.

The British, meanwhile, came up with a plan to bring the rebellion to an end. The biggest troublemakers were the New Englanders. If those colonies could be crushed, the rest would cave in. They decided on a three-pronged plan to cut off New England. Dashing General Burgoyne would lead an army south from Canada, down Lake Champlain, and along the Hudson River to Albany. General William Howe would bring troops up the Hudson River from New York to meet them. Another army, led by Colonel Barry St. Leger, would sail down the St. Lawrence River, land on the shores of Lake Ontario, and approach Albany from the west.

Burgoyne began his move in the summer. His troops, red-coated British regulars and Hessians in plumed hats, were guided south by Indian scouts. Traveling with them were the wives and children of officers and enlisted men. They crowded onto ships and, with oars splashing and sails raised, glided across Lake Champlain behind the Indians in their birchbark canoes.

The British advance started off with a huge victory. They found the one weakness in formidable Fort Ticonderoga—an unprotected summit above the fort that the Americans believed could not be scaled. During the dark of night, the

❖ The Stars and Stripes ❖

Featuring 13 stripes and the British Union Jack, our first national flag showed our ties to Great Britain. On June 14, 1777, the Continental Congress adopted a new design: 13 red and white horizontal stripes and 13 stars on a blue field. The stars were "a new constellation" in the world's nations.

Philadelphia's seamstresses went to work making flags. Many years later, Betsy Ross's grandson claimed George Washington asked her to make the first flag. There is no proof that the story is true (actually, Washington was not in Philadelphia at the time), but Betsy Ross was a patriot and may have been one of the earliest flag makers.

To honor our flag, we follow these practices:

Never let the flag touch the ground.
Raise it rapidly and lower it ceremoniously.
Fly the flag from sunrise to sunset (and never in
    bad weather), with the stars always in the
    upper left corner.
Fly it at half-mast in times of national mourning.
Display it on state and national holidays and
    special occasions—especially on Flag Day,
    June 14th.

redcoats cut a road to the top. By morning, they had dragged their heavy guns and ammunition to the steep summit. When the Americans saw British cannons pointing their way, they quickly evacuated; Fort Ticonderoga was in British hands once again.

Back in England, King George was ecstatic. He ran into the queen's bedroom shouting, "I have beat all the Americans!" Washington was downcast. "This stroke is severe indeed," he wrote. In France, the news discouraged Ben Franklin. He was there to enlist French aid and support against Great Britain. Though the French sympathized, they had no wish to side with a loser, and King Louis refused to receive Franklin.

The First Flag

St. Leger, with an army of red-coated soldiers and Mohawk Indian warriors, advanced from the shores of Lake Ontario. Fort Stanwix stood between them and their goal. St. Leger's troops placed the fort under siege. The determined Americans inside showed their resolve by hoisting a makeshift flag stitched from a white shirt, a red petticoat, and a blue military jacket. Patriots marching to the fort's rescue clashed with St. Leger's troops in a fierce and bloody battle.

August 16, 1777: Battle of Bennington

Burgoyne's troops, now traveling on land, moved south at a snail's pace. The dense and dark wilderness thwarted their every step. They pushed through the forests, hacking out trails and building bridges across marshes. Supply wagons for the thousands of troops and their followers,

★ ★ ★ ★ ★ A C T I V I T Y ★ ★ ★ ★ ★

Be a Betsy Ross

The American flag displayed 13 stripes and 13 stars. These were symbols that were flown to show that 13 new states had become part of the world's nations. (Today's flag has 50 stars, one for each state of the Union.)

Flags mean different things to different people. Interview a few people and ask how they feel about the American flag. What kinds of memories and experiences does it bring to mind? Ask a war veteran (if you don't know any veterans, visit your local American Legion or Veterans of Foreign Wars). Ask a young child. Ask someone from another country. Finally, ask yourself: What does the American flag mean to me? Find symbols that represent your thoughts and feelings and make a flag collage.

What you need
Old magazines, postcards, maps, and photos
(ask permission!)
Scissors
Poster board
Glue

After you've given some thought to what the flag means to you, go through the collection of old magazines, postcards, maps, and photos. Look for red, white, and blue images that represent what you feel about the Stars and Stripes. Cut them out and arrange them on the poster board in the shape of the flag. Glue the images to the poster board.

carrying food and ammunition as well as luxuries, bumped and jerked along the makeshift roads. Burgoyne alone had 30 wagons of belongings. He didn't intend to do without his champagne and feather bed, even in the wilds of America! (Even Washington preferred his own furniture and brought a special fold-up four-poster bed to war.)

The extra baggage and followers slowed the army's march. Local militiamen added to their problems by felling trees and pushing boulders across the few roads. These patriot militia groups gained extra volunteers when Indian scouts accompanying Burgoyne captured and scalped a young woman, Jane McCrea. The act outraged the Americans. They felt the British were turning the Indians against them. Burgoyne had been confident that loyalist supporters would flock to his army as he moved through the land. Instead he found himself in a hostile country, with supplies shrinking.

Hoping to secure new horses and supplies, Burgoyne sent 800 Hessian soldiers to the town of Bennington. Their commander, who didn't speak English, had been assured that the local people were loyalists and would help them. As the Hessians neared Bennington, they saw armed farmers in the fields. Believing the farmers were loyal to the Crown, the Hessians weren't alarmed. Soon they discovered their mistake.

The armed farmers were patriot militia; American colonel John Stark was their leader. He pointed his sword at the Hessians and shouted to his men that they would win this battle "or

Molly Stark is a widow!" By the end of the fight, nearly all of Burgoyne's men had been killed or taken captive.

Out in the west, British colonel St. Leger was nervous. He didn't want to face Benedict Arnold, who was advancing his way. Arnold had cleverly spread false rumors that he led an enormous force. St. Leger thought he was in for it. He abandoned his siege and retreated. In spite of these setbacks, Burgoyne was convinced that the master plan could still succeed. But where was General Howe?

September 11, 1777: Battle of Brandywine

General William Howe had made other plans. The official orders directing him up the Hudson River had never reached his headquarters in New York. Though he could have easily brought his army to Albany, he thought Burgoyne could handle the region on his own. Instead, Howe prepared to bring his troops against the rebel capital, Philadelphia. His soldiers and their horses boarded waiting ships and sailed out of New York.

The ships disappeared over the horizon. General Washington anxiously waited and watched, wondering where Howe was taking his army. The British could end up anywhere on the eastern seaboard. When the fleet was

spotted in Chesapeake Bay, Washington immediately guessed Howe's plans—Philadelphia was the target!

Swiftly, Washington marched his soldiers to Philadelphia. Patriots lined the streets to cheer them on. Loyalist residents peeked from behind curtains. The hodgepodge army, in plain clothes and hunting coats, their caps adorned with evergreen sprigs, marched through town and beyond to meet Howe's forces. They made camp near the banks of Brandywine Creek. For three days, all was quiet.

The calm was suddenly shattered early one morning. British fire bombarded the center of the American camp. While the roaring artillery kept the patriots busy, British general Howe and Lord Cornwallis led other troops upstream. They crossed Brandywine Creek and came up behind the Americans. The Continental Army was threatened from behind. Washington tried to fight on both fronts but soon was forced to call a retreat.

Hundreds of Americans had been killed, wounded, or captured. The losses mounted even higher the next week when the British destroyed an American camp, Paoli, during a ferocious midnight raid.

After the Battle of Brandywine, Howe marched and countermarched his troops—first one way, then another—to confuse and tire the pursuing Continentals. He finally steered his army to the village of Germantown and made camp, sending Lord Cornwallis forward with a force to take Philadelphia. On the streets where only weeks ago the homespun Americans had passed, British and Hessian soldiers marched to the music of "God Save the King."

October 6, 1777: Battle of Germantown

The Americans made one last effort to drive the enemy away from Philadelphia. In the fog of early morning, they streamed into the village of Germantown and surprised the British soldiers as they huddled around their fires. At first the redcoats scattered. The Americans shouted in triumph. They celebrated too soon. The battle deteriorated in fog and confusion, and the attack failed to destroy Howe's army. Shortly afterward, the British general moved his headquarters to Philadelphia and settled in comfortably for the winter.

In the north, Burgoyne's army struggled through the wilderness. Their slow progress gave the Americans plenty of time to prepare for them. Washington sent soldiers and officers north to meet the invaders; General Philip Schuyler worked to make them ready. In spite of his efforts, a worried Congress appointed General Horatio Gates to take his place. Militiamen, too, gathered to help. Daniel Morgan, a tall, broad Virginian, led 500 picked riflemen to help fight Burgoyne's army. These expert shooters, dressed in buckskin and moccasins, knew how to fight

Indian-style, moving stealthily through the country-side to surprise their enemy.

October, 1777: Battles and Surrender at Saratoga

The Americans braced themselves for a fight near the town of Saratoga. They built fortifications in a strong position on Bemis Heights. From the heights, their guns pointed down on river and road. The British couldn't pass by; they would be forced to fight or retreat.

When his army neared Bemis Heights, Burgoyne chose to fight. His advance guard approached the fortifications and entered a clearing in the forest called Freeman's Farm. All was silent, except for the gobbling turkeys in the trees bordering the clearing. Suddenly, the redcoats heard the crack of rifle fire—they were under attack! Daniel Morgan's riflemen were perched in the trees and crouched behind fences, signaling to each other with turkey calls.

Continental forces and more British troops came to the clearing. Soon a raging battle swayed back and forth. The Americans pushed the British back into the forest, only to have them charge forth again. As soon as the British thought they had finally overcome the rebels, the Americans found new strength. As night fell, Hessian reinforcements helped the British regain the field.

After this close battle, Burgoyne had his men dig trenches nearby and waited for help from General Howe. It never arrived. Howe was already settled down for the winter in a fine Philadelphia home. While Burgoyne worried and waited, supplies dwindled and the sick and wounded cried out for treatment.

For more than two weeks, the armies were within shouting distance of each other, but the only fighting was within the American camp. Its commander, Horatio Gates, and Benedict Arnold were feuding.

Benedict Arnold was a bold and fearless fighter. Washington believed him to be the most "active, spirited, and sensible officer" in his army. But somehow things never seemed to go right for him. Though he'd fought brilliantly in many battles, Arnold wasn't rewarded with the recognition and rank he felt he deserved. Now, after the fight at Bemis Heights, Gates didn't give him credit in a report to Congress about the battle. Gates and Arnold argued about the report. Arnold became so angry that Gates relieved him of his command and ordered him to remain in his tent.

With his army getting weaker by the day, Burgoyne realized he must either fight now or surrender. To force a way through, he sent a detachment (a special force) crashing against one end of the American line. The British were driven back in a stormy battle. When Benedict Arnold heard the crack and roar of muskets and cannons, he leapt to his feet and ran out of his tent. "Come on, boys!" he shouted as he raced

Surrender of General Burgoyne at Saratoga

Yankee Doodle

Yankee Doodle came to town,
A-riding on a pony.
He stuck a feather in his hat
and called it macaroni!
Yankee Doodle, keep it up!
Yankee Doodle, dandy!
Mind the music, and the step,
And with the girls be handy!

British redcoats loved to taunt the Americans by singing "Yankee Doodle." This was not a very nice song! Some think the word *Yankee* came from a common Dutch name (*Janke*) and was meant as a mocking nickname for the settlers of New England. *Doodle* was a word meaning "simpleton." *Macaroni* was a fancy hairstyle of the era, as well as a nickname for the dandy who wore his hair that way. American soldiers took the sting out of the insult by adopting the song for themselves.

❖

Rebus!

A rebus was a kind of a puzzle popular with 18th-century kids. They used pictures, numerals, and letters to represent words, usually using pictures of objects whose names have the same sounds as the words represented. For example, George Washington's rebus name might look like this:

They did it for fun, but it's a good way to use your imagination—and a fun guessing game for the reader.

It's not as easy as it looks to make up rebus puzzles. See if you can write a whole rebus-style letter to a friend.

George

ton

A Yankee Doodle rebus like this:

Yan- Doodle came to a-riding on a po- stuck a in his and called it

to the battlefield. His horse was shot beneath him, then he was shot in the leg, but he continued to lead his men in the fight.

The day ended with heavy losses for the British. Burgoyne ordered his army to withdraw under cover of night. In a heavy rain, they retreated to Saratoga, where the Americans surrounded their camp and kept up a steady barrage of fire. As Burgoyne gathered his officers to discuss their next move, a cannonball crashed onto the table where they sat. A brief flicker of

hope came to him when he heard that British forces under General Clinton were near, but soon even that faded. Dressed in his finest uniform, Burgoyne surrendered his army to Horatio Gates. As British and Hessian troops stacked their arms, an American band played "Yankee Doodle."

When news of the victory traveled across the country, patriot spirits and hopes rose again. The surrender inspired poems and songs, and a dance called "Burgoyne's Surrender" became a popular request at balls. In France, Ben Franklin was finally granted an audience with King Louis XVI.

General Gates ordered an officer to carry the glorious news to the Continental Congress. The officer stopped along the way. He couldn't resist a side trip to see his steady girl. By the time he delivered his message, the news was 12 days old. Samuel Adams made a motion to grant the officer a pair of spurs, and all rejoiced.

November, 1777: The United States of America

When the British captured Philadelphia, the Congressional delegates escaped to a nearby town, bringing their work along. They'd been laboring for months over a basic constitution for a national government. The newly joined states needed a government, and quickly. Without one, they couldn't make foreign alliances and decisions about money and trade or properly conduct the war against the British.

A committee led by John Dickinson drafted a document called the "Articles of Confederation." Dickinson presented the Articles to the other delegates, then left to go to war. (Though he had originally opposed the rebellion and refused to sign the Declaration of Independence, Dickinson was one of only two delegates who fought.)

John Dickinson

Dickinson's draft proposed a strong central government, and it started a heated and long argument among the delegates. Many were worried about creating a strong government. They were, after all, rebelling against one they felt had abused its power. After months of debate, they decided on a weak national government that would leave most of the power with the states. Because some states (such as Virginia) had larger populations and greater wealth than others, they decided that each state would have an equal vote. That way, one state could not overpower the others.

It took more than a year for the Continental Congress to adopt the Articles of Confederation.

It took four more years before all the states ratified (approved) them. Congress used the Articles, in the meantime, as a working constitution.

The Articles of Confederation put Congress in charge of a national government that could wage war and make treaties. But there were flaws in the document. Their concern about creating an overly powerful government caused the delegates to overlook other problems. Now they had a national government with no power over the state governments or their citizens. This caused a problem right away. The new government could not force the states to pay taxes. Congress could only ask for money and often did not get anything. And money was desperately needed.

Winter, 1777–1778: Valley Forge

Washington wrote letter after letter to Congress, begging for supplies for his suffering army. In December he brought his men to Valley Forge, high ground 18 miles northwest of Philadelphia, to wait out the winter. It took a week's march to get there through wind, snow, and sleet. When they arrived, their hardships had just begun.

In the best of times, the life of a Continental Army soldier was a difficult one. Long marches, disease, battle wounds, and primitive medical treatment took a dreadful toll. Worst was the constant hunger. The search for something to eat was the "business that usually employed us," as one private described it. At times, the only food the soldiers had was what they "borrowed" from a farmer's fields or hunted up in the woods. Washington complained bitterly about the poor rations and lack of supplies, angrily declaring that his men were made of flesh and not stone.

Now his men were wearied from their march and had no food, but they needed shelter from winter's cold. They set to work building rough log and mud huts. Washington refused the comfort of a house until the huts were finished. "I will share in the hardship and partake of every inconvenience," he said. It hurt him to see his men "without clothes to cover their nakedness, without blankets to lie upon, without shoes." Barefoot sentries stood watch while standing on their hats. Others, without shirts or coats, walked through the camps huddled in ragged blankets. One night a "dinner party" was held in camp, and only those without a pair of trousers were invited to attend.

Men suffered from frostbite. Many fell to the diseases that raged through the camps: smallpox, typhus, typhoid, dysentery, pneumonia. They were weakened by hunger, surviving on "fire cakes" (flour and water patties baked on hot rocks) and pepper soup (made of water and peppercorns). Many became angry and began to speak of revolting against their commanders.

The shortages and hardships seemed even more bitter to those who knew that food and supplies were near. Profiteers took advantage of the army's need by charging high prices. Farmers

Baron von Steuben at Valley Forge

sold goods to the British, and were paid in solid pounds (the money of England), rather than to the Continental Army, whose money was not worth the paper it was printed on. During the cold months, soldiers froze while barrels of shoes, stockings, and clothing sat along the roads, without horses or men to carry them to camp.

Only miles away in Philadelphia, the British troops were comfortably housed. General Howe turned down the chance to strike at Washington's weakened forces. Instead he enjoyed fine foods,

balls, and the company of Philadelphia's loyalist households. He held a reputation as a great soldier from earlier days but now showed no eagerness for war. Card games and dances kept him up until the wee hours of the night. According to Ben Franklin, Howe had not taken Philadelphia. "I beg your pardon," Franklin said, "Philadelphia has taken Howe."

In the terrible winter at Valley Forge, 2,000 Americans died. Many despaired and deserted, but most remained faithful to their cause and

65

❖ Foreign Aid ❖

Baron von Steuben was one of many foreign soldiers who sailed the Atlantic to fight for the patriot cause. Some came for glory and military rank. Others were inspired by America's dream of independence.

Baron Johann de Kalb, like von Steuben, was a "pretend" baron. This German peasant did much to encourage France to aid the American cause. He was given the rank of major general and in return bravely gave his life in battle.

Thaddeus Kosciuszko, of Polish gentry, came early on to assist the Americans. This military engineer designed fortifications at West Point and at Bemis Heights near Saratoga.

The Marquis de Lafayette, a 19-year-old French aristocrat, was forbidden by King Louis XVI to join the Americans. The young Marquis disobeyed. He bought his own ship, sailed the Atlantic, and hurried to Washington's side, where he served with no pay. He became one of Washington's most trusted aides and dearest friends. When Lafayette suffered a leg wound at the Battle of Brandywine, Washington instructed the surgeons to "treat him as though he were my son."

Count Casimir Pulaski proved his bravery as a hero of Poland's uprising. In America, he fought courageously at the Battle of Brandywine and gained a cavalry command. In a battle outside Savannah, Georgia, Pulaski was fatally wounded as he led his men in a courageous assault.

Marquis de Lafayette

their general. When spring came, they left their windowless huts, ready to fight again. It was a different army from the one that had stumbled into the camp at Valley Forge. The soldiers had a renewed loyalty to their general, who had suffered with them and cared for them. And, thanks to the work of Baron von Steuben, they were prepared to fight.

Von Steuben was one of many foreigners who joined the American fight for independence. He came to General Washington from Germany with a letter from Ben Franklin, who introduced the bearer as "the Baron von Steuben, lately a lieutenant general in the king of Prussia's service." In fact, the bearer was neither a baron nor a general, but he turned out to be one of the best things to happen to the Continental Army. Von Steuben volunteered his services and took on the task of training and drilling the soldiers. Under his direction, the untrained fighters became disciplined and effective troops.

The short, stocky baron began his day at 3 o'clock every morning. There was plenty to do. There seemed to be no order or discipline in the American camp. (Washington said his men "regarded an officer no more than a broomstick.") Training was haphazard and infrequent. Men came and went, often taking their muskets with them. Records were not kept, equipment not cared for, and the soldiers, as the baron quickly learned, had their own ideas. "In Europe," the baron wrote a friend, "you say to your soldier 'Do this' and he does it. Here I am obliged to say 'This is the reason you ought to do it.'"

Baron von Steuben

Von Steuben brought out the best in the independent Americans. He didn't speak English, so he memorized orders to fix bayonets, load and fire, move from column into line, and conduct other maneuvers. When angry, he swore furiously in French and German, then turned to his interpreter and asked him to swear in English on his behalf. The baron held inspections, parades, and reviews. At night, he stayed up planning drills for the next day and writing a detailed military manual. For his hard work, he was rewarded with the rank of major general in the American army.

By spring, thanks to Nathanael Greene, the tireless new quartermaster (officer in charge of equipment), the men had food, clothes, and supplies. The army also had a new ally—France. Britain and France were longtime enemies. The French had been secretly sending military supplies to the Americans for some time but held back on declaring war. Ben Franklin, sent to the French Court by the Continental Congress, helped to win France's support. He completely charmed the French people with his wit, his good nature, and his rustic fur hat. The surrender at Saratoga was the victory needed for France to officially join forces with the new United States. (Later, Spain and other European countries would declare war against the British, too.) King Louis furnished money, arms, soldiers, and sailors to the cause. To celebrate the French alliance, a grand parade was held, with Baron von Steuben organizing special drills and ceremonies. All cheered as cannons boomed and muskets fired a "feu de joie" ("fire of joy"), a running fire up and down the ranks. After a winter of suffering, the Continentals were heartened, drilled, and ready to fight.

Continental Army Classifications

1 company (or platoon) = 25 to 50 men
4 to 8 companies = 1 battalion
2 battalions = 1 regiment
2 regiments = 1 brigade

Commissioned Officers
(rank appointed by the army)
Major General
Brigadier General
Colonel
Lieutenant Colonel
Major
Captain
Subaltern (Lieutenant, Ensign)

Noncommissioned Officers
(rank appointed by a commanding officer)
Sergeant
Corporal

General Putnam leaving his plow

five

"Johnny Has Gone for a Soldier"

Homespuns, Hessians, and Redcoats

"I was plowing in the field about half a mile from home," wrote Joseph Plumb Martin, "when all of a sudden the bells fell to ringing and three guns were repeatedly fired in succession down in the village." Fourteen-year-old Joseph ran to see what the commotion was all about. A recruiter was in his Connecticut village, enlisting men for the army. Boys and men gathered in a noisy crowd, jostling to see who would step forward to join. Each dollar the recruiter placed on a drumhead was snatched up by an eager volunteer.

Joseph eyed the dollars and regretted his youth. His grandfather had forbidden him to "go for a soldier." Within a year, though, he signed his name to six-month enlistment papers and joined General Washington's Continental Army.

When the war began, there was no army. Those Americans who first gathered outside Boston in 1775 were militiamen from nearby farms and villages. Militiamen were citizen-soldiers organized to fight for their communities in an emergency. In the early years of the colonies, all able-bodied men from age 16 to 65 were required to serve in their local militia. Fearful of Indian war parties and pirate raids, they drilled several times a year to prepare for an attack.

When war became a reality, Congress created the Continental Army and appointed Washington its leader. At that time, the volunteers who joined the Continental Army signed on for short-term enlistments, hitches of six to eight months. Soon it became clear that the war would

69

last much longer than that. Washington pleaded with Congress for longer enlistments. By the time he had his soldiers trained, their time was up and they left, walking for home. Congress set new enlistments for three years or for as long as the war lasted. Men were offered a bounty (land or cash) to join. Each state was charged with supplying a certain number of men, but Congress didn't have the power to force the states to fill their quotas. There was always a shortage of soldiers.

There were 100,000 to 150,000 men who enlisted in the Continental Army (some enlisted for a short hitch, then signed up again for the duration of the war). Close to 75,000 more served in militia units. Not all of these soldiers served at the same time. The greatest number of men that Washington commanded at one time was somewhere near 17,000, a combination of regulars and militiamen.

The militiamen defended their towns and coasts against British raids. Armed with their own muskets and tomahawks, they also reinforced the Continental troops. Sometimes they caused confusion on the battlefield because they weren't as well trained as the regular soldiers. These independent men objected to the drilling and toil endured by the Continental soldiers and weren't fond of answering to authorities, but they had plenty of enthusiasm for the fight.

The soldiers came from small New England villages; the towns of Philadelphia, Boston, and Charleston; southern plantations; and the great wilderness to the west. They were tradesmen and farmers, freedmen and slaves. One clergyman, in the middle of a church service, threw off his gown and stood dressed in uniform before his congregation. More than 150 of them joined him as he marched to war.

Some saw military service as a way to a better life. Black slaves were promised freedom for enlisting. Others joined for the bounty, a plot of land at war's end. Most, black and white, sacrificed their youth, their health, and sometimes their lives for the cause of liberty.

As the years of war went on, more manpower was needed. Men in their 60s and boys as young as 12 served in the Continental Army and militia. The boys became drummers or helped the cooks in camp. Women and their children traveled with the army, too. Thousands of women served in the camps as cooks, laundresses, and nurses. They carried water and ammunition to the troops in battle.

A few women even disguised themselves as men to enlist. One, Deborah Sampson, served as Private Robert Shurtleff. This sturdy farm girl camped, marched, fought, and convinced her entire regiment that she was a young boy. To keep her family from looking for her, she wrote home saying she had found work with a "large but well-regulated family." When Deborah was wounded in battle, she crawled off into the woods and treated the injury herself rather than risk a doctor's examination. Later, she became very ill, and the tending doctor discovered her secret. Deborah was given an honorable discharge. As she stood by her general's side, dressed in a gown and

✤ Blacks Fight for Freedom ✤

One of the first to die for the American cause was black sailor and one-time slave Crispus Attucks, who lost his life in the Boston Massacre. Two blacks were among the minutemen when shots rang out in Lexington, and blacks, freedmen and slaves, served courageously in battles throughout the war.

The cause of freedom was naturally dear to their hearts. Early on, when blacks were not permitted to join the Continental Army, the British promised freedom to those slaves who would leave their masters to fight for the Crown. Thousands escaped and crossed to British lines. Some received their hard-won freedom; others were forced back into slavery. Eventually, the Continental Army offered freedom to northern slaves who enlisted. Slaves and free black men signed up. Approximately 5,000 blacks fought in the American ranks.

Black civilians guided troops marching through unfamiliar territory. They spied on British movements and plans. Pompey Lamb, posing as a farmer selling goods to British soldiers, learned the secret password to British-held Fort Stony Point. He gained entry with the password, "The fort is our own," and helped American soldiers invade and capture the stronghold. James Armistead spied on British officers as he waited on them and reported back to the American camp. British general Cornwallis was so taken in by Armistead that he asked him to spy on the Americans!

It is a sad and terrible contradiction that patriots went to war for their liberty while slavery existed in their own country. When Patrick Henry asked, "Is life so dear or peace so sweet as to be purchased at the price of chains and slavery?", he answered himself with a resounding NO!—"Give me liberty or give me death!" Yet he and many other leaders owned slaves. Abigail Adams saw the problem quite clearly: "I wish most sincerely," she wrote, "there was not a slave in the province; it always appeared a most iniquitous scheme to fight ourselves for what we are daily robbing and plundering from those who have as good a right to freedom as we have."

bonnet, her regiment paraded by. Not a single soldier recognized her.

The American troops faced a trained and professional army thought to be the best in the world. Across the field of battle they saw the redcoats advance, step by step, shoulder to shoulder, in rows two or three deep. "Fire!" the British officers shouted. The lowered muskets blasted one volley, then another.

The British regulars were a very different type from the American soldiers. A good number were drafted from England's jails and slums. After years in the service, they were tough and disciplined. Their upper-class officers demanded the strictest obedience.

With King George's empire behind them, they were better fed and supplied than the American soldiers. Their scarlet coats were made of wool and decorated with colored facings, piping, and lace. They wore stiff leather collars, white crossbands on their chests, tall black hats on their powdered heads, and white breeches.

At its peak, the British army in North America numbered 50,000. Alongside the king's red-coated troops were the soldiers from Germany called Hessians. George III hired these soldiers from German princes. Their princes benefitted; the soldiers themselves received no pay. The use of these foreign soldiers added to the bitterness American patriots felt against King George.

About 30,000 Germans sailed the Atlantic to fight in North America. Told that they would be sold into slavery if captured, they were especially fierce fighters. Their uniforms were blue and white. Most wore tricorn hats; others wore brass miter caps—tall, peaked caps that made them look large and menacing. With their heavy boots, rattling swords, and a reputation for ferocity, they struck fear in the hearts of their enemies.

Young frontiersman and surveyor George Rogers Clark vowed to bring an end to Indian raids and the British presence in the northwest. He gathered nearly 200 buckskin-clad riflemen and set off down the Ohio River to destroy the western British outposts that supplied the Indians.

Clark and his men, nicknamed "The Long Knives," quickly captured the supply posts of Kaskaskia and Cahokia (in today's Illinois), then Vincennes and its wooden fortress, Fort Sackville (in present-day Indiana). Clark befriended the French traders who lived in the western wilderness and negotiated a truce with the chiefs of the local tribes.

When he heard of Clark's successes, British lieutenant colonel "Hair Buyer" Hamilton went on the warpath. He led hundreds of redcoats and Indian warriors to Vincennes, which Clark had left guarded by only a small garrison (military force). Hamilton recaptured Vincennes but decided to wait until spring to attack Clark at Kaskaskia.

Clark refused to wait. He led his small band on a brutal 200-mile winter march to Vincennes. An early thaw had flooded the rivers and countryside. By day, the men splashed through the cold water; at night, they slept in it. They waded in waist-high icy slush, their aching arms holding powder and guns overhead to keep dry. They were freezing, wet, hungry,

George Rogers Clark's march against Vincennes

and exhausted, and only Clark's will kept them going. He sang at the top of his lungs, whooped like an Indian, and shouted encouraging words of dry ground ahead. Finally, they reached solid ground near Vincennes.

Clark sent a bold message ahead, stating his intention to capture the fort that very night. He marched his men in circles around the settlement to make it appear as if his numbers were strong. His riflemen aimed carefully at the redcoats on the fort's walls. Alarmed, Hamilton surrendered. For the rest of the war, the region was spared from Indian raids.

In Pennsylvania and New York, isolated settlements were destroyed by the loyalist Butler's Rangers and Indian warriors led by Mohawk Thayendanegea (known to whites as Joseph Brant). Entire villages were burned in sudden and savage raids.

General Washington sent John Sullivan to stop the raids. He instructed Sullivan to destroy the Indians' crops so they would have nothing to live on. Sullivan's soldiers destroyed the Indians' crops, and animals and homes, too. "There is not a single town left in the Country of the Indians," Sullivan reported. Unlike Clark's success in the west, Sullivan's efforts led to more raids. The tribes were hungry for revenge. The British continued to supply them, and for the next few years, they attacked the region's settlements mercilessly.

Joseph Brant (Thayendanegea)

An encounter between enemies

Native Americans fought on both sides. Some, including a tribe of Oneida Indians, joined forces with the Continental Army; most fought with the British. They had been threatened by the Americans, who pushed them out of their lands. This war could be a way to reclaim their territory or at least prevent the Americans from taking any more. Warriors from the Creek, Cherokee, Mohawk, and Seneca tribes fought with the British and acted as their scouts.

Supplied with British guns, powder, and tomahawks, Indian warriors attacked forts and set-tlements across the frontier. Their raids left burnt cabins and few survivors. With the scalps of conquests hanging from their belts, they journeyed to Fort Detroit. Here, British lieutenant colonel Henry Hamilton (nicknamed "The Hair Buyer") gave a bounty for each American scalp.

American loyalist regiments also fought alongside the British. Approximately 20,000 Americans fought for the Crown. They formed regiments such as the "Queen's Rangers," the "Loyal American Regiment," and the "Royal Guides and

Pioneers." Other loyalists joined special militia units or acted as spies and guides.

Early on, the untrained Americans were at a disadvantage against these forces. But by the time they left Valley Forge, Washington's ragtag men were a real army. The infantrymen memorized each step of von Steuben's drills. The artillerymen trained in the use of cannons and shot. Cavalrymen mounted on swift horses spied, patrolled, and acted as the army's advance guard. An engineer corps took on special projects, such as creating tunnels or digging entrenchments (earthen barriers with trenches behind them).

It was a special honor to be chosen for the Light Infantry Corps. This was the advance guard of the army. Its men had been personally instructed by Baron von Steuben. Later, the Marquis de Lafayette was placed in command of this elite corps. He was so proud of them he gave each a special helmet made of hard leather, decorated with a bear pelt, and topped with a red and black feather.

For much of the war, the nickname "Homespun" accurately described the Continental Army. Uniforms were hard to come by. Even some officers had to make do with civilian clothes. Washington knew his men would feel more like soldiers if properly clothed, but money and uniforms were scarce. Dressed in his own blue-and-white uniform and large three-cornered hat, he cut a magnificent figure. Other well-dressed officers displayed rank by wearing epaulets (ornamental fringed shoulder pads) on their shoulders and red silk sashes around their waists.

The soldiers did their best with their everyday clothes or uniforms that varied greatly from state to state and from one regiment to another.

At first brown was the official color of the Continental Army; later it was blue. Early on the men were fitted with breeches and stockings; later they wore long leggings. At one point it was so hard to identify American soldiers that Washington ordered them all to wear evergreen sprigs in their hats to distinguish them from civilians. One Hessian soldier was surprised to see how the Americans were clothed. "Yet no fault could be found in their military appearance," he wrote. "They are erect and soldierly…slender, fine-looking and sinewy…and a pleasure to behold."

The backwoods riflemen showed up for war with their rifles, powder horns, hunting knives, and tomahawks. They wore long, fringed hunting shirts, deerskin breeches and leggings, and beaded moccasins. Their practical shirts were good for cold and hot weather, with fringes that shed rain and snow. Because of their practicality, many others adopted the hunting shirt.

Washington soon discovered another reason to adopt these backwoods clothes. The riflemen were excellent marksmen, accustomed to hunting swift game in dark, dense forests. British redcoats, in comparison, were easy pickings. The best riflemen were sent out as scouts and snipers. The very sight of them made British soldiers nervous. The British called them "shirt-tail men" and "the most fatal widow-and-orphan makers in the world." Washington played on this fear by dressing many of his soldiers in fringed hunting shirts.

General Daniel Morgan, a rifleman

Make a Fringed Hunting Shirt

Want to be a "shirt-tail man"? Belt this fringed hunting shirt at the waist and wear with pants and moccasins. Don't forget your tricorn hat!

What you need

Linen or cotton cloth, 1½ yards by 2 yards

Long-sleeved shirt to use as a pattern (find one that is big on you—the fringed hunting shirt should come to about the middle of your thighs)

Pencil

Scissors

Needle and thread

Pins

Sewing machine (optional)

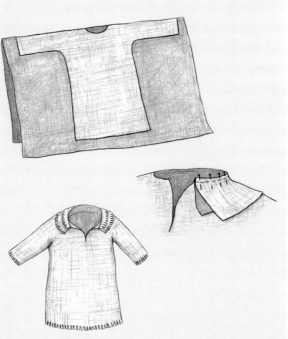

Fold the cloth in half lengthwise and spread it out on your work space. Lay the shirt over the cloth so the shoulders and tops of the sleeves lie along the fold (as shown). Use the pencil to draw around the outside of the shirt on the cloth. Make a line for the collar, too. Put the shirt away and cut along the lines through both layers of cloth. Cut along the collar line. Through one layer of the cloth, cut a line from the center of the collar down about 4 inches. Sew up the sides of the shirt and the insides of the sleeves.

Cut two strips from the leftover cloth, each ¾ yard long. One should be 5 inches wide and the other 3 inches wide. Pin the two strips all the way around the collar, with the 3-inch strip as the middle layer (as shown). Sew the collar and the two strips together.

Turn the shirt and the strips around the collar out. Cut slits, about ½ inch wide and an inch long, all along the bottom of the shirt, at the wrists, and on each of the strips around the collar.

It was a welcome moment when France came to America's aid. France sent not only soldiers and sailors but also uniforms and supplies. New blue coats with white facings, buff-colored breeches and waistcoats, black three-cornered hats, and shoes came across the ocean. (The shoes weren't made to fit left and right feet but were all the same. They took some breaking in!) The French soldiers were a colorful addition to the camps. Some dressed in white uniforms with green facings, others in light blue jackets, yellow breeches, and fur capes. Several regiments wore white and rose, with white and rose feathers on their hats. Others marched to battle in dramatic black and white.

Brown Bess and Battle

Officers carried swords and, sometimes, espontoons (long staffs with spearheads). When an officer returned to his tent, he stuck his espontoon in the ground at its door to let everyone know he was in. Officers and cavalrymen also carried pistols.

Artillerymen brought their big guns to the battlefield behind horses or oxen borrowed from farmers. In battle, they furiously loaded and fired their cannons, howitzers, and mortars into enemy ranks and strongholds. They used solid cast-iron balls of different sizes or loaded the guns with grapeshot (a cluster of small iron balls) or canisters filled with musket balls.

One King = 4,000 Pounds

A lead statue of King George that stood in New York was torn down by the Sons of Liberty. Melted down, it provided 4,000 pounds of lead—enough to make 42,228 musket balls for the Continental troops.

✤

Most of the Continental soldiers fought with muskets, from the "Militiaman's Fowler" to the British "Brown Bess" and, later, a French infantry musket. The common Brown Bess was a heavy, 4½ foot, smoothbore musket that fired ¾ inch balls. Loading and firing was a time-consuming task and hard to do in the heat of battle. The soldier ripped the end of a paper cartridge with his teeth and poured powder into a firing pan. The rest of the cartridge, holding powder and ball, went into the musket's barrel and was stuffed in with a ramrod. He returned the ramrod to its place, brought the gun to his shoulder, cocked the firelock, aimed, and fired. Flint sparked in the powder-filled pan; a charge ignited in the barrel. The ball flew out but often missed its target. The musket was only accurate within about 80 to 100 yards.

The riflemen used the Pennsylvania or Kentucky Rifle, a more accurate weapon. The long rifle had a ridge inside the barrel that sent the ball spinning in a direct and deadly flight. These rifles took longer to load and held no bayonet but had a range accurate at 250 to 300 yards.

Most weapons were so clumsy and inaccurate that the soldier had to be very close before shooting. He looked his enemy in the face. Often, orders were given to hold fire until the soldiers could see the buttons on the British soldiers' uniforms or "the whites of their eyes." Even at such close range, it was easy to miss. After several volleys, the soldiers resorted to a bayonet charge or hand-to-hand combat, clubbing with musket butts and fighting with fists.

European officers were trained to conduct a certain type of war. It was considered ungentlemanly to use unexpected tactics. War was supposed to be like a chess game, with rules and customs to observe. Generally, American officers followed the same customs, but sometimes their opponents felt the Americans were breaking the rules. With the capture of Philadelphia, for instance, the English thought they'd checkmated the Americans. Yet, even though the seat of their government was occupied, the rebels did not come forward to surrender. They continued to fight.

Opponents were supposed to meet in the open, on a field of battle, and execute maneuvers understood by both sides. The American army also fought by these rules; most battles occurred in the open, with armies at close range. Some Americans knew how to fight Indian-style and fought using trees and hills for cover. After their training under Baron von Steuben, they used the best of both European and American fighting tactics. American riflemen ignored the unspoken rules and aimed their guns at British officers. Civilians broke the rules, too, firing on British troops and spying on their movements.

Though British troops captured cities and won battles, the Continental Army never gave up. Because he generally had fewer men, Washington had to fight smart. He used strategy when he couldn't use force. Washington sent his men out in small groups to attack quickly and withdraw. They conducted surprise attacks, then evaded and outmarched their confused enemy.

Retreat from Concord

✤ Bold Women ✤

Women worked in the army's camps. At home, they supported the army by making bullets, sewing clothes and blankets, raising money for supplies, and spying on enemy movements. They protected their homes and communities with muskets and pitchforks.

Buckskin-clad "Mad Anne" Bailey rode her horse Liverpool across the frontier to recruit soldiers. She also acted as a scout and messenger.

Teenager Sybil Ludington, "the female Paul Revere," rode swiftly through the Connecticut countryside to warn her neighbors of a British attack.

Young Beth Moore carried a secret message to an American officer. With a friend and her small brother, she rowed a boat right past British sentries into the American camp. British soldiers thought the children were simply playing.

Vermont's Hannah Hendee crossed a deep river in pursuit of Indians who had kidnapped her children. Though threatened with tomahawks, she wouldn't leave until the chief gave them back. She carried her children across the river, then went back to rescue her neighbors' children! The Indians were so amazed at her courage that one man offered to carry her across the river. She accepted.

Several women received the nickname "Molly Pitcher" for carrying water to wounded soldiers. The most famous Molly was Mary Ludwig Hayes, who went to war with her husband, an artilleryman. When her husband was wounded, she bravely took his place at the cannon.

It went against Washington's nature to fight in this way, for he was a bold and aggressive general who liked to take risks. But in this war, Washington knew that the best thing he could do was keep his army together long enough to wear down the British. He hoped King George and the people of England would get tired of war.

Hardship: A "Constant Companion"

It was a wonder that the American people did not tire of war before the British. The British thought most Americans were against the war. Many of them were. Quakers and other pacifists refused to fight. Some people just didn't want to take sides. Others, firmly loyalist, sided with the British. Families and neighbors came to hate and distrust each other. Communities were torn apart by political beliefs. Some loyalists were placed under arrest. They were whipped or tarred and feathered, and their houses were burned. Their property was taken away from them. Many loyalist families left their homes and moved behind British lines for safety or left the country altogether for Canada or England.

With fathers and brothers in the army for so long, women and children shouldered all of the work. They plowed fields, tended animals, and planted and harvested crops. They learned to hunt in order to feed their families. Many civilians suffered greatly from shortages, which became worse as the war went on. Clothing and food were scarce, and money lost its value. "A wagon-load of money will scarcely purchase a wagon-load of provision," wrote Washington. Farms were devastated as passing armies foraged for food and seized precious horses and cows. Raiding British soldiers set crops on fire; families watched as a year's worth of back-breaking labor went up in flames. Some, like General Philip

Schuyler's wife, Catherine, burned their own crops rather than allow the British to feed off them. Their homes were taken over. At times, battles raged on their doorsteps. Whole towns were burnt to ashes, and people searched through the rubble for any small token of their lives. The armies left the dead and wounded in their wake.

Passing armies also spread diseases throughout the civilian population. Diseases raged throughout the armies and treatment was poor; 10 times as many soldiers died of illness than in battle. They suffered from typhoid fever, pneumonia, malaria, scurvy, and smallpox. Doctors and nurses used herbal remedies or resorted to primitive medical treatments such as blistering (believed to draw the disease out) and bloodletting (which only served to weaken the patient). A crude inoculation against smallpox was developed: a needle was drawn through an infected smallpox pustule, then inserted into the skin of a healthy soldier. The inoculation didn't always work and sometimes just spread the disease.

"Our constant companions were fatigue, hunger, and cold," said Joseph Plumb Martin. It is amazing that he and so many others did not abandon the cause. The soldiers were supposed to receive a daily ration of bread, meat or fish, and vegetables, but there were frequent shortages. A piece of hard biscuit and a bit of salt pork seemed like a feast. One hungry soldier was told by his colonel to settle for a piece of burnt Indian corn "and learn to be a soldier!" As a special holiday treat, Continental Army troops were issued "half a gill [¼ cup] of rice and a tablespoonful of vinegar."

Many soldiers had never been away from home before. They worried about their families. They felt lonely, too, surrounded by men from other states (a man from Massachusetts considered a Virginian a "foreigner" and vice versa). Fights often broke out between soldiers from different regions, and guards were posted to preserve the peace in camp. Washington did his best to get rid of these distinctions and asked the men to think of themselves as Americans.

In winter camp, there were plenty of things to do other than fight. The soldiers with tents would set them up or make makeshift tents of blankets to live in until they could build log huts. They also built hospitals, kitchens, a parade ground for drills, and special cabins for the officers. They cleaned their weapons, made cartridges, and drilled. They gathered wood, carried water, and cared for the animals. When they had time to themselves, they sewed their clothes, whittled pipes and toys, engraved powder horns, or went off to forage for food. For entertainment, they listened to the music of camp musicians, put on plays, and ran races.

When they were called to "ready—march!" the men picked up their 10-pound muskets, cartridge boxes, a haversack containing food and a tinderbox, and a canteen made of wood. Their knapsacks were stuffed with blankets and other equipment—perhaps a pipe, a little money (very little, for the soldier was paid less than seven dollars a month), or some fishing gear. They

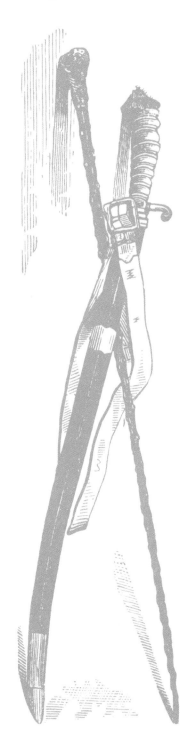

Hauling guns by ox teams

took turns carrying the heavy cast-iron kettles that were assigned to each "mess" (a group of six men who ate together). It was easy to track the Continental Army, British soldiers said, by the abandoned kettles along the roads.

In hot summer weather, men suffered from the weight of their burdens and heavy clothing. On rainy nights, they huddled together and tried to keep their muskets and powder dry. In the cold, they awoke covered with frost. During the winter, some suffered frostbite, and their poor, frozen feet had to be amputated. On night marches,

in cold weather and in wet, with stomachs shrinking against their backbones, they crossed roadless miles. Exhausted men fell asleep while marching.

When they met the enemy, officers bellowed commands and drums beat signals. In the heat of battle, wounded men and horses screamed, rifles cracked, artillery boomed. Young Joseph Martin, in his first experience of war, said when shots were fired he "made a frog's leap for the ditch" and wondered "which part of my carcass was to go first."

Create a Powder Horn

Soldiers used the hollow horn of an ox or cow, fitted with a cover, to carry their gunpowder and keep it dry. Make yours from papier-mâché.

What you need

12-inch square of poster board

Tape

Scissors

Newspapers

½ cup flour

1 cup water

Bowl

Spoon

24 inches of string

Glue

Paints and paintbrush

Old rag for cleanup

Roll the poster board into a cone and tape it to hold its shape. Trim the wide end so that it is even. Lay some of the newspapers over your work space. Cut about 8 pages of newspaper into 2-inch strips. Mix the flour and water in the bowl and stir until smooth.

Cover the cone with layers of newspaper strips that have been dipped in the pasty mixture. Make the powder horn curved up at the end by twisting little strips at its narrow end. Let it dry overnight.

Cut a round lid for the wide end of the powder horn from the leftover poster board. Tape it to the horn. Glue the ends of the string to each end of the horn. Let it dry.

During long winter days in camp, soldiers carved expressions, decorations, and their names on their powder horns. Paint your horn white with a black tip, then decorate it with sayings such as "Liberty or Death!," your name and the date when you made the horn, or a list of the battles you've fought.

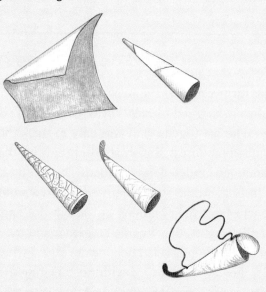

Sew a Pouch

No rifleman went without his pouch and powder horn (to carry gun powder), lead (for making bullets), and other necessities.

What you need
½ yard of felt (brown for a realistic look)
Chalk
Scissors
Needle and thread

With the chalk, draw a long oval on the felt (you can use your foot as a rough pattern, as shown in the picture). Cut out the oval. Use this piece to trace a half-oval on the felt, then cut that out.

Cut a long strip from the remaining felt, about 1 inch wide.

Sew the two pieces together around the outside edges (as shown). The other half of the full oval will serve as the pouch's flap. Sew each end of the strip to the sides of the pouch.

The wounded soldier faced another dangerous enemy—medical treatment. There was no anesthetic provided for surgery. When doctors performed amputations or removed musket balls from wounds, the only relief the patient could get was biting on a bullet. Because doctors did not understand the cause of infections, they used dirty instruments and did not wash out wounds.

Both sides treated prisoners very badly (though officers got better treatment). Americans were held in prisons, in church crypts, and on British ships. These floating prisons were dreadful places, where men were kept below decks, were fed wormy bread and worse, and died by the thousands of smallpox and yellow fever.

Joseph Plumb Martin wrote that "almost everyone has heard of the soldiers of the Revolution being tracked by the blood of their feet on the frozen ground. This is literally true, and the thousandth part of their sufferings has not, nor ever will be told." Still, he said, "We were determined to persevere." He showed his resolve by reenlisting and served to the end of the war.

"The World Turned Upside Down"

June 28, 1778: Battle of Monmouth Courthouse

One hot June day, the British army packed up and left Philadelphia. Their new commander, Sir Henry Clinton, had orders from London to move his headquarters to the safer haven of Manhattan. The American alliance with France had shocked England. A French fleet was on its way to the Atlantic shores! Soon after the redcoats began their march to Manhattan, the Continental Army left Valley Forge to follow them.

Hot weather, thunderstorms, and heavy baggage slowed the march. The British lines straggled along the country roads. The perfect opportunity to strike, thought Washington. His second in command, General Charles Lee, disagreed. He had just returned after months as a British prisoner and perhaps had seen too many well-trained and armed redcoats. Lee discouraged the attack, saying there was no chance the Americans could stand up against the British regulars.

Lee's strong opinion swayed Washington for a few days. Rain continued to muddy the roads; hot temperatures followed, and soldiers collapsed with heatstroke. Washington could no longer resist attacking the vulnerable army. He gave Lee the command to attack when Clinton stopped near Monmouth Courthouse.

The Americans started off boldly, but, with Lee in command, they soon fell apart. Lee attacked carelessly, ordering his men forward, then back. He failed to send support to units in trouble. Finally, he ordered a retreat. Just then, Washington rode up to see how his troops were faring. He was shocked to find them in retreat.

Battle of Cowpens

Washington relieving General Lee

"What is the meaning of this, sir?" Washington demanded. Lee replied that "the American troops would not stand the British bayonets." "You never tried them!" cried Washington. While cannon fire exploded around them, Washington reprimanded Lee so severely that a bystander said, "He made the leaves shake on the trees." He ordered Lee off the field of battle.

Disheartened by the retreat and exhausted by 100-degree temperatures, the patriot soldiers had collapsed in a nearby forest. Washington spurred his white charger and rallied them to battle. Inspired, they advanced and fought until darkness fell. In the dark of night, Clinton withdrew his troops and led them to Manhattan.

The British reached Manhattan safely. Even the newly arrived French admiral d'Estaing, with his fleet of magnificent ships and 4,000 troops, was unable to stop them. A joint effort between the French and Americans to dislodge the British from Newport, Rhode Island, also failed. The commanders quarreled, a hurricane sent

✤ John Paul Jones ✤

(1747–1792)

Bold American captain John Paul Jones invaded the British coast and attacked a castle! (Later, he sent an apology to the countess.) He cruised the English Channel, firing on ships. One evening, he spotted a British convoy sailing in the North Sea. Though the convoy's warship, the *Serapis,* outgunned his *Bonhomme Richard* (named for Benjamin Franklin's *Poor Richard*), Jones attacked.

As Jones neared the *Serapis,* its captain shouted, "What ship is that?" "Come a little nearer and I will tell you!" roared Jones. The ships engaged, firing broadsides that shook them bow to stern. They collided and stayed locked together for the length of a terrible battle. Men fought with guns, spears, and fists; the decks became slippery with their blood. *Bonhomme Richard* caught fire, its hold flooded, and it began to sink. The British captain called on Jones to surrender. "Sir," Jones retorted, "I have not yet begun to fight!" The sea battle raged for two more hours. Finally, under the light of the moon, the British captain lowered his flag in surrender.

the ships in all directions, and d'Estaing set sail for the West Indies.

Though this attack failed, the French sea-power was welcome. The Continental Navy started with four used merchant vessels armed with cannons, then added 13 frigates (one proudly christened the *Hancock*). Even as the navy grew to more than 50 ships, it was not equipped to fight Admiral Lord Richard Howe and the superior Royal Navy. With 270 warships bristling with cannons, Britain's navy had the ability to blockade American ports, threaten coastal towns,

and give support wherever the British army needed it. Just that year, British warships had fired on coastal Connecticut towns, burning one to the ground. England's cargo and merchant ships were the British army's lifeline, bringing additional supplies and soldiers across the Atlantic Ocean.

To weaken that lifeline, about 800 privateers (armed private vessels) went to sea on behalf of the United States government. The captains hired their own crews and paid them with the spoils of captured ships. Over the years, they seized thousands of British merchant ships.

The War Moves South

Washington felt encouraged when General Anthony Wayne captured Fort Stony Point on the Hudson River. With a hand-picked detachment, Wayne invaded the stronghold at midnight. Though wounded, Wayne insisted his men carry him inside to receive the British commander's surrender in person.

On the other side of the ocean, King George and his advisors were frustrated. There was little to show for the long years of war. They had been unable to crush the northern colonies. It was time to take the war to the South. They believed that many southern loyalists would flock to the king and fight alongside the redcoats. Southern plantations could feed the British troops. And while they conquered the South,

West Point

Washington would be stuck in New York, keeping Clinton's army in Manhattan. The colonies would fall like dominoes. It seemed like the perfect plan, especially in late 1778, when British forces captured Savannah, Georgia, without a hitch. Within a month, Augusta fell, too, and soon all of Georgia was under British control.

American general Benjamin Lincoln did his best to take Savannah back. He called on the help of French admiral d'Estaing, who landed his fleet on the Georgia coast. Together they demanded that the British surrender, but Savannah's defenses were strong and the redcoats were prepared for a fight. A dawn attack failed after a short, fierce struggle. There were few British casualties but many French and American losses. The Polish count Casimir Pulaski died of battle wounds, after bravely and repeatedly charging the British at the head of his cavalry command.

Back north, as winter set in, Washington sent some of his army to West Point to hold the strategic Hudson River against invasion. With the rest of his soldiers, he settled into winter quarters at Morristown, New Jersey.

Though the winter at Valley Forge became most famous for its hardships, the winter of 1779–80 was the worst of the century. A blizzard prevented the men from building huts, then deep snows collapsed their tents right on top of them. More than 20 snowstorms followed until the snow was packed six feet deep, making it impossible to forage for food. Bitter cold set in. "It was cold enough," wrote Joseph Plumb Martin, "to cut a man in two." At one point, Martin had nothing to eat for four days except some birchbark he gnawed off a branch. His friends roasted and ate their shoes.

Clinton kept busy during that cold winter. In February, with thousands of soldiers and General Cornwallis, he landed near Charleston, South Carolina. General Lincoln and his patriots held Charleston as long as they could but surrendered after a six-week siege. The loss of Charleston was a devastating blow, the worst of the war so far. Five thousand soldiers, the entire southern Continental Army, were taken prisoner. Tons of supplies were seized.

Shortly after this terrible loss, a few hundred American militiamen near the village of Waxhaw

Casimir Pulaski

into battle shouting "Tarleton's Quarter!," a battle cry meaning to give no mercy.

Battle of Camden

August 16, 1780: Battle of Camden

Clinton returned to the rest of his army in New York. While he was gone, a French fleet with 5,000 soldiers under Comte de Rochambeau had landed at Newport, Rhode Island. Still, Clinton felt confident that the war was going well. He had left the southern command in the hands of Lord Cornwallis. Once a member of Parliament who had voted against taxing the colonies, Cornwallis now led an army against them. He intended to subdue the colonies from south to north and began by building a chain of forts in South Carolina. Congress ordered General Horatio Gates—the hero of Saratoga—to stop him.

Gates failed miserably at his task. He lost many of his men on a brutal march to Camden, South Carolina. They inched forward through swamps and wilderness in the heat of the southern summer. They had little food and only bad water to drink and fell by the hundreds to disease and hunger. When they finally faced their enemy, the Americans—mostly new recruits—threw down their arms and ran. Horatio Gates ran faster than any of them.

Some soldiers bravely stood their ground. One was Baron de Kalb, a German volunteer

were suddenly attacked by Tarleton's Legion, a cavalry command under Lieutenant Colonel Banastre Tarleton. The overwhelmed Americans raised a white flag in surrender. The battle should have ended then with Tarleton accepting the surrender and taking the men prisoner. Instead, according to American accounts, he ordered his troops to slaughter the patriots. Tarleton became the most hated of British officers. Americans nicknamed him "The Butcher" and "Bloody Ban." After that, patriot militia went who refused to give up. He and his men charged the British lines again and again. De Kalb was wounded 11 times before he fell. As his men raced back through the swamps, they were ridden down by Tarleton's Legion.

September 23, 1780: "Treason of the Blackest Dye"

Benedict Arnold was in love. While acting as military commander of Philadelphia, he met, and later married, Peggy Shippen. Peggy was young, beautiful, charming, and a Tory. Other American officers were suspicious of Arnold's relationship with the loyalist Peggy and unhappy about his questionable money-making schemes. Arnold lived in the finest house in town and threw extravagant parties for loyalist guests. He was charged with misconduct and found guilty of minor offenses. Washington, who thought Arnold a good officer, gave him the gentlest of reprimands.

Washington's trust was misplaced. For months, Arnold had been slipping coded messages to British general Clinton. In exchange for money and a title, Arnold offered his services to the Crown. He told secrets about troop movements and plotted to hand the strategic fortress of West Point, with its 3,000 soldiers, over to the British.

✤ Francis Marion, "The Swamp Fox" ✤
(1732–1795)

After the Battle of Camden, a guard of loyalist soldiers marched Continental prisoners off to prison camp. Suddenly, shots rang out. The guard was under attack! The prisoners broke free and their captors ran, unaware that their attackers were just a meager band of 17 men.

The defeat at Camden devastated the patriot army, but Colonel Francis Marion united a band of partisans and kept fighting. Like other bands under Thomas Sumter and Andrew Pickens, Marion's men camped in the swamps and swept out on daring raids against the British and their Tory allies. Their hit-and-run attacks kept the redcoats on edge. "They will not fight like gentlemen," complained a British officer, "but, like savages, are eternally firing and whooping around us by night and by day waylaying and popping at us from behind every tree."

Frustrated Banastre Tarleton, unable to capture Marion, cried, "This damned old Fox, the devil himself could not catch him!" For two years, Marion and his band of partisans (which never numbered more than 100) hid in the swamps; ambushed enemy camps, patrols, and supply lines; and thoroughly annoyed the British command.

Arnold pleaded with Washington for the command of West Point. Washington granted his request. As soon as he took over command, Arnold set about weakening West Point's defenses. He drew detailed plans of its entrances and gun placements and sent them to Clinton's adjutant (assistant), Major John André.

As the scheduled British takeover approached, André and Arnold arranged a midnight meeting to go over the scheme. Their plans set, André rode away with secret documents hidden in his boot. He carried a pass signed by Arnold, giving permission for its bearer—"John Anderson"—to travel.

Washington happened to be nearby. He sent word to Arnold that he was coming to inspect West Point's fortifications. As Arnold sat down to breakfast that morning, he received another

Benedict Arnold

message saying that a spy named John Anderson had been captured. Arnold's secret papers betraying the cause were on their way to General Washington! Knowing that the penalty for treason was death, Arnold said a hurried good-bye to his wife and newborn son. He rowed downriver to a British ship and sailed off to safety.

Arnold's treachery shocked the nation. Patriots everywhere hanged and burned his likeness. Major André was tried and hanged for the crime of spying. Arnold, who had been one of America's finest officers, now fought for the British. He even led troops against his own hometown and burnt it to the ground.

Benedict Arnold's Secret Code

Benedict Arnold and John André sent their secret messages using a number code. They wrote the messages to look as if they were business transactions between merchants. That way, anyone who might see the messages wouldn't be suspicious of the lists of numbers. No one wants to be a Benedict Arnold, but it's fun to send messages in code!

What you need
A friend or family member
Paper
Pen
2 dictionaries (you and your accomplice
    must each have the same kind)
Candle
Matches
Adult help suggested

First, write out your message. Then convert it to a number code. Look up the first word of your message in the dictionary. Write down the page number that the word appears on. From the top of the page, count down the number of lines until you get to the word. Write this number down. Dictionaries usually have words listed in columns on each page. Write down the number of the column where the word appears. These three numbers together represent the word. (For example, "Beware" might be written as "34.9.3".) Continue for the rest of your message.

Arnold and André folded their letters and sealed them with wax. Light the candle and carefully drip some of the wax onto the letter to seal it shut.

Nathanael Greene
(1742 – 1786)

With no military experience or formal training, Nathanael Greene became one of the greatest patriot generals. While working as a blacksmith and miller, Greene taught himself history, mathematics, and (in spite of his pacifist Quaker upbringing) military science. Greene started as a private in a Rhode Island militia company. One general said that within a year he was "equal in military knowledge to any...and very superior to most." As quartermaster general, Greene saw that the men at Valley Forge were fed. As southern commander, Greene's creative strategies surprised and confounded his enemies.

October 7, 1780:
Kings Mountain

In the South, after the defeats at Charleston and Camden, only small groups of patriot militia survived to fight. Cornwallis confidently moved his army across the countryside, sending word ahead that mercy would be granted to those who swore allegiance to King George.

British major Patrick Ferguson, an expert marksman and hardy commander, recruited loyalists to fight under the king's banner. With a well-drilled force of 1,000 loyalist and British forces, Ferguson marched to the western Carolina mountains, burning patriot farms along the way. Their actions enraged the independent frontiersmen who had settled in this region. They gathered together to oppose Ferguson. These patriots, called "overmountain men," rode swiftly over the hills, dressed in fringed hunting shirts and carrying long rifles. Ferguson warned them to "desist from their opposition" or he would "hang their leaders, and lay their country to waste with fire and sword." The overmountain men seethed with anger.

Joined by North Carolina and South Carolina militia, the overmountain men closed in on Ferguson. Ferguson moved his force to Kings Mountain, while the pursuers, led by Colonel William Campbell, followed through a dark night's driving rain. They fought their way up the slopes in a short but furious battle and swept over their enemies. Ferguson was killed at the front of the fight, his men surrounded and destroyed.

As the war raged through the South, no mercy was shown on the battleground and no mercy granted to civilians in the armies' paths. British troops and southern loyalists looted patriot homes and burned their crops. Patriots took revenge, torturing suspected loyalists. Loyalist families left everything they owned and traveled hurriedly away from danger. Patriot women cried as their husbands were torn from their arms. When Washington sent General Nathanael Greene to take charge of the war in the South, Greene was appalled by the destruction and bloodshed. "I have never witnessed such scenes," he wrote.

When Greene arrived at the army's camp in Charlotte, North Carolina, he found only a hungry and ragged militia force of 2,000. They were untrained, but Greene thought they had spirit enough to fight. "We're going to fight a war, not march in a parade," he said grimly.

January 17, 1781:
Battle of Cowpens

All military teachings of the time advised against a weak army splitting up when facing a stronger enemy. Greene threw tradition aside and divided his very small force. While one wing made camp near the South Carolina border, 600 soldiers under Daniel Morgan marched to the west. Greene hoped that Cornwallis would respond to this move by sending a detachment against Morgan. Perhaps they could beat the British one piece at a time.

Cornwallis took the bait, sending Banastre Tarleton with his force of 1,000 to stop them. When Greene learned of Tarleton's approach, he sent word to the tall, buckskin-clad Morgan that "Colonel Tarleton is said to be on his way

Banastre Tarleton

A C T I V I T Y

Reenact the Battle of Cowpens

What makes a great military leader? Courage, brains, and a great plan. Daniel Morgan had them all. Get your friends together and reenact the Battle of Cowpens.

What you need
A bunch of friends—12 or more
Red ribbons
Evergreen sprigs
Safety pins
Sticks (pretend guns)

Choose sides. The British soldiers should tie red ribbons around their arms. The patriots should identify themselves by pinning evergreen sprigs to their clothing (as the real patriots did).

"Daniel Morgan" should line his troops up in three lines. Place the best sharpshooters in a line in the front. Give them orders to shoot, then have them race around behind the last line. Behind the sharpshooters should stand a line of militia.

Morgan was sure the militia would run, so he ordered them to do so—but only after firing three volleys. Tell the militia that, after three shots, they should race away and re-form in the rear. Behind the militia waits a line of Continental soldiers and cavalry (horse soldiers) under "William Washington" (George's cousin).

The battle begins. "Forward, march!" and the redcoats should advance, in step and shoulder to shoulder. When the sharpshooters fire, several redcoats should fall. The rest still march forward. Then the militia fire once, twice, three times! A few redcoats should fall.

While the British soldiers continue forward, the militia and sharpshooters run around and behind the last line. In the smoke of battle and confusion, the British are sure that all of the Americans are running away. The British advance once again, right into the line of cavalry and Continentals. It's a trap! The battle ends with the British all taken prisoner.

to pay you a visit. I doubt not but he will have a decent reception."

The forces met at the Cowpens, a cattle-grazing ground in South Carolina. The night before Tarleton's "visit," Morgan walked through camp teasing and encouraging his men. With his surefire battle plan, he felt confident. He placed his sharpshooters in front, the militia in a second line, and his very best troops in the back. The first two lines would shoot, then fall back, to lure the British forward. When the redcoats got closer, they would meet the battle-tested cavalry and Continentals.

At sunrise, Tarleton attacked. Morgan's plan worked. The redcoats rushed up to the third line without realizing the trap. The battle was over in an hour, a British disaster.

March 15, 1781: Battle of Guilford Courthouse

After Cowpens, Greene led an angry General Cornwallis on a grueling chase across North Carolina and into Virginia. Greene stayed one march ahead of the British, buying time until he could gather more recruits and get ready to fight again. Until then, he wore out the British by drawing them through the forests and across the rivers of North Carolina. The red-coated soldiers dropped, exhausted and running out of food.

Cornwallis ordered his men to torch their own wagons and equipment. From now on, they would travel fast and light. Still, they could not catch Greene's army, and with each march they were farther from their supply reserves on the coast. They raided the countryside for food and forage, angering the local people. Just as the American army was within reach, Cornwallis lost them. They crossed a river into Virginia, taking every boat along. Cornwallis threw up his hands and turned back into North Carolina.

Several weeks later, Greene marched back into North Carolina. Reinforced with Continental soldiers and new militia recruits, he was ready to face Cornwallis.

At Guilford Courthouse, while cavalry commander "Light-Horse" Harry Lee held Tarleton's horsemen back, Greene readied his troops for battle. Worried about his unpredictable militia, he set them in lines similar to those at Cowpens. His first line of militiamen were instructed to slow the advance of the redcoats with two solid volleys. On either side and behind them were more experienced cavalry and infantry. Holding the last line were seasoned Continental soldiers.

The militia fired, then fled in the face of the advancing redcoats. Lee saw them "throwing away arms, knapsacks and even canteens, rushing like a headlong torrent through the woods." Out of the smoke, the redcoats advanced, stepping over their fallen comrades. Here, toward the second line in a dense forest, the struggle was furious. "I never saw such fighting since

Cornwallis

Battle of the Guilford Courthouse

Two Famous Lees

The fearless, hotheaded Henry ("Light-Horse Harry") Lee led a crack cavalry unit called "Lee's Legion." In their bearskin crested caps, white breeches, and green jackets, they rode hard and struck fast. In his private life, Lee was a rich planter who loved horses, cards, and fancy clothes. This hero of the American Revolution became the father of another famous American—Robert E. Lee, commander of the Confederate forces in the Civil War.

✤

At the battle of Eutaw Springs, hundreds of my men were naked as they were born. The bare loins of many were galled by their cartridge-boxes, while a folded rag or a tuft of moss alone protected their shoulders from being chafed by their guns.

—General Nathanael Greene

God made me," Cornwallis said. The battle raged back and forth until patriot cavalry lunged into the fight. Cornwallis ordered his artillery to fire into the fray, on Americans and Britains both, to end the fight. Greene ordered a retreat.

It was a British victory but a deadly one. Cornwallis's outnumbered army lost twice as many men as Greene's. "Another such victory," said one member of Parliament, "would ruin the British army."

Cornwallis ordered his men to the British-held town of Wilmington, North Carolina, to re-supply, then marched them off to Virginia to join other waiting British troops. He would concentrate on conquering Virginia, hoping that the rest of the South would then admit defeat. He sent Tarleton to attack Charlottesville, where he nearly captured Thomas Jefferson and Patrick Henry. Cornwallis raided Jefferson's estate and burned his home and crops. The Marquis de Lafayette, in Virginia with a small force, did what he could to annoy and divert Cornwallis. Under General Clinton's orders, Cornwallis looked for a safe place along the coast to fortify as a base.

His forces took over Yorktown, near the Chesapeake Bay, and began to build fortifications.

Meanwhile, Nathanael Greene moved off to seize other British posts in the South. He cut off the supplies of a garrison at Hobkirk's Hill and called on partisan fighters to take over forts in South Carolina and Georgia. At the oddly named Ninety Six, South Carolina, his soldiers placed a fort under siege, withdrawing only when British reinforcements approached. At Eutaw Springs, South Carolina, Greene led a dawn attack against a British encampment. The raid almost worked, but the ragged American soldiers, some nearly naked, stopped to plunder their enemy's tents and baggage. The British regrouped and counterattacked. Both sides claimed victory, but the British suffered more losses. By the end of the year, only Savannah and Charleston were still held by the British. Greene, without winning a major battle, had nearly regained the South. "Without an army, without means, without anything [Greene] has performed wonders," wrote American general Henry Knox.

October 19, 1781: Surrender at Yorktown

After months of inaction outside New York, Washington could hardly stand the frustration. "The cause is lost and my country is ruined!" he cried. Finally, he talked French commander Comte de Rochambeau into joining him against General Clinton's New York encampment. Rochambeau's soldiers marched in from Rhode Island, and the two commanders began plans for a siege. Their plans changed when they received word that a French fleet, originally expected to arrive near New York, was closing in on Chesapeake Bay.

French admiral Comte de Grasse had set sail, with 28 ships and 3,000 men, toward Yorktown. If he could hold Chesapeake Bay, Cornwallis could not escape by sea, nor could reinforcements land to help him. If Washington and Rochambeau could move quickly enough, they might be able to surround Yorktown by land and together defeat Cornwallis's army.

First, they had to get away without letting Clinton know their plans. Washington tricked him by marching his army toward New York. He ordered his soldiers to build encampments and big brick ovens, as if they were preparing for a long siege. He had his officers ask known loyalists for directions to places far from their real destination and planted false secret messages with spies. Then, leaving a small force behind, Washington and Rochambeau made their way to Yorktown. Fooled, Clinton was sure the French and Americans were about to attack New York.

De Grasse's fleet met 20 British ships off the coast of Virginia. For two hours their cannons boomed. Outnumbered and badly damaged, the British ships sailed away, leaving Admiral de Grasse in control of Chesapeake Bay. When Washington heard that de Grasse held the bay, he jumped and danced and waved his hat above his head.

Yorktown was surrounded. Cornwallis knew he was in trouble. He ordered his soldiers to prepare for a siege by building ramparts and redoubts (enclosed forts). He was relieved to get word from General Clinton that help was on the way. But could he hold out until it arrived? His troops were outnumbered nearly two to one.

The American and French soldiers furiously dug zigzag trenches and built redoubts until they were close to Yorktown's walls. They brought up artillery to bombard the town. Virginia governor Thomas Nelson suggested they fire on his own Yorktown home first. He thought Cornwallis might be headquartered there and offered a reward to the first artilleryman who struck the house.

The French and Americans bombarded the town. British artillery returned fire. Shot and shells crossed in the air, and buildings and ships caught fire. Deafening noise from nearly 100 big guns pounded, day and night. All the while, soldiers continued to dig trenches until they slowly encircled the town.

Surrender at Yorktown

Two British redoubts held up the advancing trench diggers. Alexander Hamilton led an American brigade against one; a French brigade was assigned to seize the other. "Rochambeau" was the password for their attacks. The Americans liked that because it sounded to them like "Rush on, boys!" They rushed the fortifications and overpowered the Hessians and British holding the redoubts.

Inside Yorktown, supplies were running short. The desperate British tried to make a midnight escape by boat. The attempt failed when a huge storm swept in. Cornwallis began to despair, giving up on the hope of reinforcements from Clinton. "It is no good! The game is lost!" he cried.

The relentless bombardment went on for nine days. Then one bright morning, a red-coated drummer boy stepped to the top of a crumbling wall. He pounded out the drumbeat calling for parley (a conference between enemies). All held their fire. Soon a British officer carrying a white flag came forward and was brought, blindfolded, to General Washington. He carried a note from Cornwallis. The British were ready to surrender.

Two days later, Cornwallis's army marched out of Yorktown to give up their arms. (Cornwallis begged off, claiming he was too sick to surrender in person.) They filed slowly to the field of surrender between lines of French and American soldiers. Washington rode up and down the lines, quietly ordering his men to hold back their triumphant cries. "Posterity will huzzah for us," he told them.

The French and American soldiers squared their shoulders and stood silently. Crowds of people who had gathered to watch the surrender were silent, too. They had traveled from miles around, some on horseback from nearby farms, others rafting down the York River, to witness the surrender. Men with set jaws, wide-eyed children, women with babies on their hips watched as the long war came to its end. The British and Hessian soldiers threw their weapons into a pile while a British band played an old ballad about a world turned upside-down.

If ponies rode men and if grass ate cows,
And cats should be chased into holes by
   the mouse,
If summer were spring and the other way
   'round
Then all the world would be upside down

Washington's farewell

· seven ·
A Good Peace, a New Nation

September 3, 1783: Treaty of Paris

Ben Franklin was overjoyed when the fighting came to an end. "There is no such thing as a good war or a bad peace!" he exclaimed. It took some time, though, before the war officially ended. British armies still occupied New York, Charleston, and Savannah.

In Europe, Franklin, John Adams, and John Jay negotiated a peace settlement between the warring countries. Washington kept his army near the Hudson River in case things went wrong. A year and a half later (eight years to the day since the first shots at Lexington) the troops learned that a peace treaty had been reached.

The Treaty of Paris set the boundaries of the United States from the Atlantic Ocean to the Mississippi River, from the Great Lakes to Florida (which was held by Spain). It also required the states to return property to loyalists who did not fight in the war.

The war had taken a terrible toll. More than 25,000 Continental Army soldiers died. (There are no accurate estimates for the militia.) Afterward, 70,000 loyalists moved to Canada, returned to England, or started their lives over in the West Indies. Around 5,000 Hessians stayed to make new homes in the United States.

101

Changed Lives

The war changed the lives of many. Loyalist families, no longer welcome in their communities, left farms and homesteads to make new lives in faraway places. The Hammill family of South Carolina had lost their father, a loyalist fighting in the king's army. Their cattle, horses, and hogs, their furnishings and tools were plundered and stolen. Mrs. Hammill drowned while trying to bring her six children to Halifax, Nova Scotia. Her oldest son, Stephen, was left to try to support his brother and sisters in a strange new country. He petitioned the British court for help, having lost all "by reason of loyalty to his Majesty during the late disturbances in America." It's likely no help was provided.

Others, like many of the Hessian soldiers, found their lives changed forever too. Hessian Jacob Rereschnick was reluctantly "drafted" into the army one day when he was threshing hay on his family farm in Germany. Seized by authorities and forced into the army, he found himself fighting for the British in America. He was wounded in his first battle—Saratoga—captured, and imprisoned. Later, he was taken in by a German-speaking American settler. He married the settler's daughter Mary. Together, they raised their five children in a log home in the new United States.

❖

December 23, 1783: Washington Resigns

By war's end, many American soldiers were angry at their government. They had gone without food, worn their clothes to rags, and left their families to fend for themselves. Now, because Congress was unable to collect money from the states, the soldiers hadn't been paid in months.

Several regiments marched on Philadelphia to demand back pay. Fearing for their lives, Congress packed their bags and marched to a nearby town. Some people wanted Washington to lead the army against Congress and take over. When he heard this, Washington said, "No occurrence in the course of the war has given me more painful sensations." He met with the unhappy officers and asked them for patience. As he reached for his glasses to read them a letter, he said, "I have already grown gray in the service of my country..I am now going blind." That remark changed their hearts, and, with tears in their eyes, the officers abandoned their plans.

When the last British forces left, the Continentals celebrated with fireworks. Washington thanked his men for eight years of devotion. "With a heart full of love and gratitude I now take leave of you," he said. "I most devoutly wish that your latter days be as prosperous and happy as your former ones have been glorious." Congress toasted him 13 times at a dinner held in his honor. Washington returned to his Mount Vernon home, refusing any pay for his wartime services.

Washington's retirement astonished the world. He could have been king of a new country, but instead he set his arms aside. History had few examples of a victorious military leader renouncing power. His act signaled that the world had changed.

September, 1786: The Annapolis Convention

Soldiers returned home to plant crops and rebuild villages. Though war had ended, life was still difficult. People struggled with heavy debts. States issued worthless paper money. Prices soared. Neighboring states argued over boundaries and charged taxes on each other's goods. The 13 states didn't act at all like a single country. France even appointed 13 ambassadors—one for each state!

States didn't pay their taxes. Most defied the Treaty of Paris and refused to return loyalist property. Great Britain wouldn't leave its frontier posts along the Great Lakes. Spain refused to allow boats through the port of New Orleans. On the oceans, pirates captured American merchant ships. Congress was powerless to do anything.

When Maryland and Virginia argued over Potomac River fishing rights, representatives

> *We had lived together as a family of brothers...had shared with each other the hardships, dangers and sufferings incident to a soldier's life; had sympathized with each other in trouble and sickness...Now we were to be, the greater part of us, parted forever...Ah! It was a serious time.*
>
> —Joseph Plumb Martin, on his last day as a soldier

from both states met at Washington's home to solve the problem. After this meeting, Virginian James Madison called for another council, of all the states, to discuss similar issues of boundaries and trade.

Before the delegates met in Annapolis, a group of angry farmers gathered in Massachusetts. Deeply in debt and losing their farms, they followed Daniel Shays in an angry uprising against the Massachusetts government. One thousand farmers blocked the courts. They tried to seize a federal arsenal and skirmished with state militia. Massachusetts asked for help, but Congress had none to give. Shays's Rebellion shocked many people. Washington worried that mob rule would overwhelm the government.

The Annapolis Convention delegates agreed they had bigger problems than questions of trade. Their weak Union was disintegrating. The Articles of Confederation, drawn up in 1777, didn't meet the needs of these troubled times. Madison and New York delegate Alexander Hamilton called for a stronger government. Hamilton proposed a meeting to revise the Articles of Confederation and Congress agreed. Delegates from the 13 states were invited to gather in Philadelphia.

May, 1787: The Constitutional Convention Meets

James Madison, ready and very eager, was the first to arrive in Philadelphia. Spring rains and muddy roads delayed the other delegates. George Washington was reluctant to leave his quiet home but knew there was important work to do. People rang bells, set off cannons, and lined the streets for a glimpse of their towering hero. Eighty-one-year-old Ben Franklin arrived in a sedan chair carried by four men. Ailing John Dickinson came to represent Delaware.

Altogether, 55 men from 12 states met for the grand convention. (Fears that a strong central government would result from the meeting

James Madison
(1751–1836)

Madison was described as "no bigger than half a piece of soap," but he had one of the greatest minds of his time. Though he was the youngest delegate in Congress, everyone listened when he spoke. His knowledge and leadership at the Constitutional Convention earned him the title "Father of the Constitution." (He disliked the title, declaring that the Constitution was "the work of many heads and hands.") He was Thomas Jefferson's best friend and secretary of state, husband to lively Dolley Madison, and fourth president of the United States.

❖

✤ Alexander Hamilton ✤
(1757 – 1804)

Alexander Hamilton was born in the West Indies and raised by a single mother. A kind employer raised money to send him to a New York school. When war interrupted his studies, he became Washington's aide and fought at Yorktown. Later, he served in Congress. With Madison and John Jay, he wrote a series of articles (now called *The Federalist Papers*) that convinced people to adopt the Constitution. After acting as Secretary of the Treasury, he continued to be a powerful political figure—so influential that he helped defeat candidate Aaron Burr (who had been Jefferson's vice president). The angry Burr challenged him to a duel. They met on the banks of a river and chose their weapons. Pistols in hand, they paced away from each other, then turned. They fired at each other. Burr's aim was deadly—Hamilton died from his wounds.

kept Rhode Island from attending. That thought kept Patrick Henry away, too. "I smell a rat!" he said.) John Adams and Thomas Jefferson, busy as ambassadors to Great Britain and France, shared their ideas in letters to the delegates.

Jefferson was impressed with the list of delegates, calling them "an assembly of demi-gods." These thoughtful and intelligent men knew that the work ahead of them would affect many generations to come. Most, like Alexander Hamilton, were young. Most had served in Congress. There were lawyers, like one-legged Gouverneur Morris, and planters, like Virginia's George Mason. There were doctors and merchants and the pres-

ident of a college. Two were modest farmers, one a shoemaker.

One-third of the delegates fought in the war. Charles Cotesworth Pinckney fought at Germantown and Brandywine Creek. His delegate cousin Charles Pinckney had been a British prisoner. Shoemaker Roger Sherman had helped draft the Declaration of Independence and the Articles of Confederation. James Wilson, born in Scotland, and Elbridge Gerry of Massachusetts (who complained so much he was nicknamed "The Grumbletonian") were among those who had signed the Declaration. Several were state governors, including Edmund Randolph and John

Rutledge. The brilliant but disagreeable Luther Martin was attorney general of Maryland. Massachusetts's Nathaniel Gorham had been president of Congress.

The delegates came and went over four months, the hottest summer of anyone's memory. Some showed up for a short time, then went home. One delegate arrived almost three months late! Some left in frustration when discussions didn't go their way, then came back later to have their say.

Philadelphians graciously offered their State House for the meeting. They spread dirt on its cobblestone street to muffle the sounds of passing carriages. Seated three or four to a table in the first-floor room, the delegates sweated and suffered through the miserably hot summer. The doors were locked and windows shut against flies—and busybodies, for the delegates vowed to keep their debates private.

In private, they could express their opinions and work things out without pressure from the outside world. James Madison took careful notes of everything that was said but promised not to publish them until the last delegate died (which happened to be him). Someone always kept an eye on talkative Ben Franklin to make sure he didn't share any details with friends.

They unanimously elected George Washington as the meeting's president. They agreed that seven states would make a quorum (the minimum needed to hold a meeting). Each state would have one vote. They would speak one at a time, with no reading, passing notes, or talking while a speaker held the floor (though there were no rules against napping!). Everyone would have a chance to speak on each topic. If someone wanted another chance to speak, he had to ask for special permission. They agreed that they could debate, take informal votes, and change their minds. Formal votes were saved for later, when everyone was informed and ready. These flexible rules kept the delegates together when they might have flown apart, for they had come to Philadelphia with many different points of view.

The Virginia and New Jersey Plans

The Convention was supposed to meet "for the sole and express purpose of revising the Articles of Confederation." Some delegates had something bigger in mind. They wanted a strong government to replace the weak confederation of states. Virginian Edmund Randolph introduced a plan for government, created by James Madison, that went way beyond the Articles of Confederation. This "Virginia Plan" proposed a national government with an executive, a court system, and a two-branched legislature (a House of Representatives and a Senate). The government would be very powerful—able to veto (cancel) laws passed by state governments. Some delegates thought it would be too powerful.

Gouverneur Morris disagreed. "Better a supreme government now than a despot twenty years hence," he said. The Virginia Plan sparked intense debates in the sweltering room. The delegates from the small states were troubled. Under the Virginia Plan, the number of representatives from each state would be based on population. The small states would be overwhelmed by states such as Virginia and Pennsylvania. Under the Articles of Confederation, each state had one vote, no matter what its population.

After weeks of argument, William Paterson proposed the "New Jersey Plan." It had a one-house legislature and a three-person presidency, and it gave each state an equal vote. It appealed to the smaller states but was rejected. And nobody wanted the plan presented by Alexander Hamilton. He suggested a model like the British government, with a president serving for life. Rumors spread that the delegates were going to invite King George's son Frederick to be king of the United States.

The delegates did agree that the best way to govern was by dividing power among different branches of government. That way, no one person or branch could become too strong. They quickly voted for a two-branched Congress. But how the states would be represented in Congress remained a knotty problem. Should each state have an equal say? Or should representation be based on each state's population or according to how much tax money the state paid? How could the small states ever get their way if they were always outnumbered? It began to feel as if the small and large states would never agree. Some even suggested erasing state boundaries and starting over.

Day after hot day, sweating in their wigs and woolen coats, they argued and talked and debated. Franklin passed his speeches to James Wilson, who stood up to read the wise old man's ideas. Everyone studied Washington's face and tried to guess what he was thinking. James Madison took down every word. At night, they talked at the Indian Queen or the City Tavern, sipped tea in Philadelphia's parlors, or sat under Ben Franklin's mulberry tree. Some delegates left town, exhausted by the heat and arguments. "We were…scarce held together by the strength of a hair," one wrote.

The Great Compromise and the Three-Fifths Rule

The delegates were creating a new constitution—an outline for government. Creating a new government was a daunting task, but they didn't start from scratch. They had studied history and political philosophy. They knew about and admired ancient republics. Several were familiar with the unwritten constitution of the Iroquois Confederacy, a tribal union that made decisions together under a Great Council. Many had written their state constitutions and used them as models. The government of Great Britain, with

Brilliant and witty Gouverneur Morris, called "the Tall Boy," gave 173 speeches during the Constitutional Convention. James Wilson spoke up 168 times and James Madison 161. A couple of delegates attended and voted but never said a word. George Washington spoke only once.

✤

The revolt from Great Britain...[was] nothing compared to the great business now before us.

—GEORGE MASON, WRITING TO HIS SON FROM
THE CONSTITUTIONAL CONVENTION

its two-branched Parliament, served as a model for the new constitution, too.

They debated over issues of power, elections, and a national executive who might be too much like a king. Mostly, they kept coming back to representation. Finally, Connecticut's Roger Sherman came up with a compromise. Each state would have one member in the House of Representatives for every 40,000 people (this number later changed). In the Senate, the states would have equal representation—two senators each. This compromise, called the "Connecticut Compromise" or "Great Compromise," saved the Convention.

The solution created a new problem. If the number of representatives depended on population, what about slaves? If slaves were counted, the southern slave states would have many more representatives and could have a greater advantage in any vote. If they weren't counted, the northern states would have more power.

The topic of slavery was a dangerous one. Many loathed slavery and wished to abolish it. Rufus King called it "a curse." George Mason, a slave owner, agreed. Gouverneur Morris said he hated to "saddle posterity" with a constitution that included it. But most of the delegates from slaveholding states said they would not agree to a constitution that interfered with the practice of slavery.

They argued and argued, set the topic aside for a while, then came back and argued again. It looked as if the states would split up if they did not compromise on this issue. They finally agreed that Congress would not pass any law prohibiting the slave trade for the next 20 years. For purposes of taxation and representation, each slave would count as three-fifths of a person.

A Government Forms

Over the next several months, the delegates created a government of three branches, each serving to check and balance the others. The legislative branch (Congress, made up of the Senate and the House of Representatives) would make laws and have the power to tax, regulate commerce, and declare war. The judiciary (the Supreme Court) would decide on disputes between states. It would also decide if any laws went against the principles of the Constitution. The executive branch would administer the

A Fatal Compromise

Without the "three-fifths rule," Alexander Hamilton believed "no union could possibly have been formed." The delegates compromised, some hoping that in time slavery would fade away. It didn't. Generations more suffered in bondage. For decades, the issues of slavery and the rights of states to govern themselves divided the nation. In 1861, 11 states seceded (left the Union) over states' rights and slavery, and the country went to war. During the Civil War, 620,000 countrymen died.

✦

government. Its leader would serve as commander in chief and make treaties.

The delegates voted dozens of times on the executive branch. At first, the idea of a single executive shocked them. They might as well have a king! But after trying on the idea of a three-person executive, they decided that one (the president) could do the job best. The president would be powerful and could veto legislation passed by Congress. To prevent that power from being abused, they decided Congress could override that veto with a two-thirds vote. They set up a system so the president could be removed from office in case of treason or other high crimes.

Ben Franklin wondered what would happen if the president died or fell ill. The delegates decided that voters should select two presidents, and whoever came in second would be vice president. (After there was a tie vote for the presidency, that system was changed.) The vice president would take over in emergencies and would preside over the Senate.

And who would vote for the president? They had already decided that the House of Representatives would be chosen by popular vote. George Mason, James Madison, and James Wilson felt strongly that the people should choose their representatives, who would speak for them. It was "a clear principle of free government," exclaimed Madison. ("The people" at the time generally meant white property-owning males. It took several amendments and many decades before freed slaves, women, and others got to

vote.) Because they believed that senators would represent the states, they decided the Senate should be elected by the state legislatures (this later changed).

The delegates considered letting Congress or the state governments choose the president. It seemed crazy to leave this choice up to the people. The country was too big and people were too spread out. How would they even know who was running for office? The delegates compromised with a system called the "Electoral College." The people and legislatures of each state would choose electors, who would in turn cast their votes for the presidency.

There was so much to do, and the summer went quickly. They had only one break (George Washington went fishing). During the months in the stifling State House, they decided on term limits (six-year terms for senators, two-year terms for representatives) and qualifications, such as age and citizenship, for elected officials. The delegates, remembering the hardships early colonists suffered because of their religious beliefs, agreed there should be no religious qualifications for office.

They determined how laws should be created and passed. They defined the powers that Congress would have and the powers of the states. Each state would honor the laws of other states, and a citizen of one state would have the rights of citizens in all others.

They decided that any new states joining the Union would have the same representation and rights as the original 13. It was possible that new

There Ought to Be a Law!

Have you ever wondered how a law is made? It starts with an idea (maybe yours!). Here's a classroom activity that shows how Congress makes laws.

What you need
A big group of kids—at least 20
Paper
Pens or pencils
Copier

Appoint one person to be president, one person to be a clerk, and divide the rest into two groups—a Senate and a House of Representatives. For every senator, there should be approximately four members of the House of Representatives. Choose a few members of each of these groups to serve on special committees. Committees can be like those in the real Congress, such as the Committees of Agriculture, Science, Education, or Energy. Or you can make up topics of your own.

One person proposes his or her idea. (This is called "sponsoring the bill" and can be done by representatives or senators.) He or she writes up the bill and gives it to the clerk. The clerk assigns a number to the bill and makes copies.

Now the appropriate House committee gets to work. If the bill is about education, the members of the education committee get copies of the bill to look over. They decide if the House will vote on the bill or if the bill will be tabled (set aside). They may want to get more information before they decide. The committee interviews experts, looks up information, and argues about the bill. If they decide to recommend it for a vote, the bill is read before the House of Representatives. The members debate and then vote on it. (Have the clerk collect the votes and keep tally.)

If the House passes the bill, it goes on to the Senate. The appropriate Senate committee looks at it carefully and does some research and interviewing, too. If they like the bill, it is read before the Senate, they debate it, and a vote is taken.

If passed by both House and Senate, the bill is sent to the president for signature. The president gets out his or her special pen and holds it over the document. The president might sign the bill and make it a law or say, "I don't think so," and veto (cancel) the bill.

Even if the president vetoes the bill, it can still become a law. If Congress votes again and two-thirds of them still say "aye" (meaning "yes"), the bill can pass without the president's approval

The Electoral College—It's Not a School

On election day, people cast votes for the president of their choice, but the president is not elected by these popular votes. When people choose a candidate, they're actually voting for state electors who elect the president.

Each state has as many electors as it does representatives in Congress. A few weeks after the general election, this Electoral College votes. If there is a tie or no clear majority, the House of Representatives chooses the president (Thomas Jefferson and John Quincy Adams were chosen this way). With some exceptions, state electors all vote for the candidate who received the majority of the votes in their state. (That means that even if presidential candidate Mary Lee receives only 51 percent of a state's popular votes, 100 percent of the electors in that state will vote for her.) Because of this complicated system, there have been times when the person with the most popular votes nationwide has lost the election.

states would join soon. Congress, still meeting in New York, passed the Northwest Ordinance to allow the lands north of the Ohio River and west to the Mississippi to form into states as they became populated. Slavery would be prohibited in these states and trial by jury and freedom of worship guaranteed.

They considered having a permanent location for the government (and decided to think about it later). They shaped a Supreme Court and decided that the president, with the approval of the Senate, would appoint its judges. And, just in case, they set up a system to make changes to the Constitution. With approval of two-thirds of Congress and three-fourths of the states, amendments could be made.

September 17, 1787: "We the People of the United States"

A "Committee of Style and Arrangement" spent four days writing up the summer's work. Gouverneur Morris did most of the work. "We the People of the United States," the document began, "in Order to form a more perfect Union, establish Justice, insure domestic Tranquility, provide for the common defence, promote the general Welfare, and secure the Blessings of Liberty to ourselves and our Posterity, do ordain and es-

tablish this Constitution for the United States of America." They wrote up their resolves in seven articles divided into sections and brought copies to the State House for the delegates to go over one more time.

They changed some details and debated about others. George Mason stood to speak. He wanted to include a list of basic human rights in the document, rights that the government would promise not to violate. Many of the state constitutions had included such a list (called a bill of rights). Mason had written one for Virginia's constitution. The delegates took a vote. They decided that it was unnecessary to outline such rights. The state governments guaranteed them, and they did not believe there was any reason to add them to the Constitution. More days of debate and revision followed. Finally, the delegates voted on the document. "All the states aye," wrote Madison.

They gathered one last time at the State House and listened as the Constitution was read aloud. George Washington spoke up for the first time and suggested a minor change (all agreed). Ben Franklin hoped everyone would sign the Constitution to show unity, but three refused. "Grumbletonian" Elbridge Gerry wouldn't sign. Edmund Randolph, who had introduced the Virginia Plan, now wasn't sure he could support the Constitution. George Mason was troubled because there was no bill of rights.

The rest lined up according to their state, from New Hampshire to Georgia. One at a time,

The United States of Jefferson

Thomas Jefferson had already thought up names for the new states that might join the Union. Some were based on Indian words such as Illinois ("tribe of men") and Michigan ("dam of twigs"), others on Greek or Latin. Imagine living in Polypotamia ("many rivers"), Pelisipa ("country of the skins"), or Chersonesus ("peninsula")!

❖

✦ Kingdoms and Commonwealths, ✦ Dictators and Democracies

Governments come in all sizes and shapes, from communist Cuba to Norway's constitutional monarchy. In a traditional monarchy, a king or queen reigns. Sultans rule their sultanates. In communist countries, resources (such as factories and farms) are owned by the public and controlled by the government. Leaders make all decisions about labor, production, and wages. Socialist governments control their country's resources in a way designed to give all citizens an equal share. In dictatorships, power is in the hands of a single military leader. In commonwealths, countries are bound together for a common good (like the British Commonwealth of Nations, which includes Australia and Canada).

Many words are used to define the United States government. We have a *constitutional government,* with a constitution that outlines our laws and rights and our government's responsibilities. We are a *democracy.* In a pure democracy, the state is governed directly by its citizens. Because there are so many people in the United States, we vote for people who will speak for us. That makes us a *republic* — a type of government in which people exercise power through elected representatives. (James Madison called this a *representative democracy.*) We are also a *federal republic.* That means we are governed by a central federal government as well as state and local governments.

they signed their names to the Constitution. Franklin, while waiting for the others, pointed to Washington's chair, which had a sun carved on its back. "I have often looked at that sun without being able to tell whether it was rising or setting," he said. "Now at length I have the happiness to know that it is a rising and not a setting sun."

Ratification

The Convention was over. It was time to share their work with the people. The Constitution would be "the supreme law of the land" if the people agreed to it. But would they?

Congress asked the states to call conventions to vote on the Constitution. Nine states had to pass it for the Constitution to be ratified (go into effect). Any state that said "no" didn't have to be

Mercy Otis Warren
(1728–1814)

Mercy Otis Warren was opposed to the Constitution and not afraid to say so. She wrote against the secret meeting, the government's power, and the lack of a bill of rights.

A poet and playwright, Warren was an unusual woman for her time. She had no formal education but learned what she could from her brothers and their tutors. (One of her brothers was patriot James "taxation without representation is tyranny" Otis.) She married a Massachusetts political leader and befriended many who played important roles in America's revolution.

Before the war, Warren wrote a play that predicted events to come. Afterward, she wrote a history of her era. At a time when most women had no voice, hers was heard.

in the Union. Copies were sent to state legislatures. Newspapers printed the whole Constitution, and people read it eagerly, line by line. They had waited through the whole summer to see how the Convention's delegates would amend the Articles of Confederation. They were shocked to find a whole new plan for government.

Everyone had an opinion and shared it in letters, speeches, pamphlets, and articles. Those who were for the new Constitution were called "Federalists." Alexander Hamilton, John Jay, and James Madison were among them. They wrote a series of supporting newspaper articles under the name Publius that came to be known as *The Federalist Papers*.

Many were against it, feeling the proposed government would be too strong. They thought that Congress should have very limited power

Interior of Independence Hall

Independence Hall

Constitutional Amendments

The first 10 amendments to the Constitution, passed in 1791, are known as the "Bill of Rights." These amendments protect the fundamental rights of United States citizens. They include freedom of religion and speech, freedom of the press, the right to peaceful assembly, and trial by jury.

Including the Bill of Rights, only 27 changes have been made to the Constitution. After a tie vote for the presidency, the Twelfth Amendment was passed to improve the election system. The Thirteenth Amendment freed the slaves. After the Seventeeth Amendment, senators were elected by popular vote. The Eighteenth outlawed the sale and manufacture of alcohol (the Twenty-first Amendment repealed the Eighteenth). Women won the right to vote in 1919 with the Nineteenth Amendment. The Twenty-sixth lowered the voting age to 18. The latest—the Twenty-seventh Amendment—took 203 years to be ratified! It states that congressional pay raises can only take effect after an election.

and that the real power should be held by the states. They were distrustful of the educated framers, who had held the long summer's meeting in secret. They were fearful of a powerful government after having just won their freedom from the Crown. These were the "Anti-Federalists." Patrick Henry was one of them. He gave passionate speeches against the Constitution, saying it would lead to monarchy.

Where was the bill of rights, Henry asked, "those essential rights of mankind without which liberty cannot exist?" Many others also wanted the answer to this question. The document defined all the duties of the government but didn't mention the rights of its citizens. Jefferson (writing from France), Samuel Adams, John Hancock, future president James Monroe, and Richard Henry Lee wanted individual rights outlined. They wanted guarantees of the right to a fair trial, freedom of religion, and freedom of speech.

The Federalists believed that the system itself would guarantee these rights and that they didn't need to be stated. Don't forget, they said, this will be your government, and you will choose who will stay in power. Why be afraid of a government when you will be electing its officials? These arguments were reassuring. Even more reassuring was Washington's support, for everyone trusted him.

Delegates were chosen and state conventions met. Delaware was the first to pass the Constitution. In Pennsylvania, some Anti-Federalists boycotted the meeting. That way there would be no quorum and no vote could be taken. Angry

Federalist Philadelphians dragged them to the State House and forced them to their seats. Massachusetts delegates were inclined to vote against the Constitution. They were especially upset about the slavery issue and that there were no religious qualifications for office. Samuel Adams had his doubts and wanted to hear more before he voted. "I came to learn," he said. Massachusetts delegates decided they wanted a bill of rights. They voted "aye," with the understanding that these rights would be added to the Constitution.

Other states followed their lead, asking that the Constitution be amended to include a bill of rights. The ninth state, Virginia, passed it in June. That Fourth of July, 1788, people celebrated with parades and parties. Ships and floats were pulled down the streets of New York and Philadelphia. Cannons and fireworks announced the ratified Constitution.

In time, all of the states became part of the Union. The old Congress gave way to a new one. In April 1789, George Washington found out he'd been elected the nation's first president. Washington left Mount Vernon once more to serve his country. John Adams came home from England just in time to become the first vice

---

★ **ACTIVITY** ★

Everyday Heroes

You probably see images and reminders of George Washington every day. He's on the quarter and the dollar bill. All across America, there are streets, towns, and rivers named for him and other important people from the time of the Revolutionary War. Here's a fun game to play wherever you are.

What you need
Paper and pencil

See how many figures from this book you can find in your everyday life. You might find them on the Washington quarter or on products such as Hancock Insurance, Samuel Adams beer, or Revereware (pots and pans). Maybe you live in Jefferson County or go to Joseph Warren Grade School. Hold a contest with your friends to see how many Revolutionary War heroes you can discover every day.

It might be hard to find heroes such as Joseph Plumb Martin, who fought as a common soldier for seven years, or women like Abigail Adams or Anne Bailey. Do you think there should be landmarks or streets named after them, too?

What Happened Next?

Twenty thousand mourners attended Ben Franklin's funeral.

George Washington served two terms as president.

A site on the Potomac River (Washington, D.C.) was chosen as the nation's capital.

John Adams became the second president.

Thomas Jefferson was elected the third president. He added 800,000 square miles to the country's territory with the Louisiana Purchase.

Alexander Hamilton was killed in a duel.

James Madison became the fourth president.

The United States and Britain fought again in the War of 1812.

Adams and Jefferson died on the same day—the Fourth of July, 1826 (the 50th anniversary of the Declaration of Independence).

Thirteen Ways to Celebrate Being an American

1. Bake an apple pie.
2. Dress in red, white, and blue.
3. Visit your local, state, or national representatives to see government in action.
4. Powder your hair.
5. Whistle "Yankee Doodle."
6. Memorize the Preamble to the Constitution.
7. Be an informed citizen—read the newspapers and watch the news.
8. Visit a battlefield.
9. Start up a fife and drum band.
10. Be like Ben Franklin—ask every morning, "What good shall I do this day?"
11. Sign your name with a quill pen (a feather with its tip cut).
12. Learn all the words to "America the Beautiful."
13. Speak your mind (and let others speak theirs).

✦

Be a History Buff

"What really happened?" Answering that question leads historians to dusty books in old libraries and letters stuffed in attic trunks. They might interview people, too, or walk an old battlefield or trail to reenact events.

Your neighborhood has a history. You can be its historian!

What you need
Paper
Pencil
Library card
Pen
Tape recorder
Blank cassette
Ruler

Start by talking to your parents, teachers, and librarians. Find out about your neighborhood. Who were the original inhabitants or settlers? Was your neighborhood settled by a particular ethnic group? Why did they pick this area? Is the same group still living in this area or have different people come?

Ask about the major streets in your neighborhood. Sometimes, roads were built over early trade routes and trails. Find out if there are any original homes nearby and ask to visit them. When were they built? Are they different from houses that are built today? Look for old buildings that might have cornerstones with dates on them. Take rubbings by placing paper over the date and rubbing the side of a pencil back and forth on the paper until the date shows. Look for monuments and do the same. Go back to the library and find out about the people or events the monuments honor.

Do you know any older people who have lived in your neighborhood for a long time? Ask your parents to help you find an older person who would like to be interviewed. Bring your tape recorder and a list of questions. Ask them to tell you the first things they remember about the neighborhood and the major events that have happened since that time. Go to the library and see if you can find proof of their stories. Your librarian can show you how to look through old newspapers on microfiche.

Draw a time line of neighborhood events, like the one at the beginning of this book. Draw a map of what your neighborhood might have looked like when it was first built and what it looks like today. Write up your findings and your original research.

The Peace Ball

president. James Madison drafted the promised Bill of Rights, which was ratified in 1791.

A revolution had occurred. It had started "in the minds and hearts of the people," said John Adams, in the years before the war. Over the years, the rugged riflemen, the hard-working farmwives, the distinguished officers, and the wise delegates had together created a new nation. It was a nation unlike any that had ever existed before. In this brand-new form of government,

power came not from a distant monarch but from the people. Its Constitution promised freedom and guaranteed the rights of its citizens down the ages.

A story was told that as Ben Franklin left the State House after the last meeting, he was stopped by a young woman. "Dr. Franklin," she asked, "what kind of government did you give us? A monarchy or a republic?" "A republic, if you can keep it!" he replied.

Since that time, the United States has grown beyond anything its founders had ever dreamt. Explorers found their way across the continent, and settlers followed them. Great wars were fought, one that nearly split the United States in two.

Through it all, the Constitution has served as a framework and guide. Franklin hoped that the Constitution would last, though he joked that "nothing in life was certain but death and taxes." Now, well over 200 years later, it is the world's oldest written constitution. It has been copied in some form by many governments, and government by the people has become common throughout the world.

Glossary

TWENTY FOUR SHILLINGS

Iffued in defence of American Liberty

Enfe petit placidam, fub Libertate Quietem

MAGNA CHARTA

Aug.t 18. 1775.

Amendment (to the United States Constitution): A formal change to the document, which can be made with the approval of two-thirds of Congress and three-fourths of the states

Anti-Federalists Those who argued against the ratification of the Constitution

Articles of Confederation The charter of the 13 colonies, adopted by Congress in 1781 and replaced in 1788 by the Constitution

Artillery Large weapons, such as mortars and cannons

Barrage Concentrated fire on a part of an enemy's line

Barrel The tube on a musket through which the musket ball flies

Bayonet A dagger attached to the muzzle of a musket

Bill of Rights A declaration of the principles of a government and the rights of individuals

Boycott To refuse to buy

Burgess A leading citizen, such as a mayor or wealthy landowner

Cartridge The Revolutionary soldier's ammunition—paper that held gunpowder and musket ball

Casualty A person killed, wounded, or captured in battle

Colony A region separate from but under the control of a parent country

Committees of Correspondence Committees set up by Samuel Adams and the Sons of Liberty in communities across the colonies. These committees kept in touch about important issues and organized responses to British acts

Common (as in Boston Common): Public land in a town, open to the use of all citizens

Confederation In this case, the group of sovereign states that combined together in 1776

Constitution The basic customs and laws that define the functions of a government

Continental A soldier of the United States Continental Army

Democracy A system of government in which the state is governed directly by its citizens

Detachment A body of troops set off on special service

Entrenchments Earthen barricades with trenches behind them

Federal government A government that divides power between a central government and subdivisions (such as states)

Federalists Those who supported the adoption of the Constitution

Firelock A device on a musket that produces sparks to set off the charge

Frigate A sailing war vessel

Galley A large rowboat

Garrison The military force defending a fort or town

Grapeshot Cast-iron pellets packed together for cannon shot

Haversack A shoulder bag carried by soldiers to hold rations

Hessians Soldiers from Germany hired to fight in America

Legislature A group empowered to make laws for a country or state

Militia Citizens enrolled and drilled in a military organization

Monarchy A government in which power is held by a single ruler, who generally inherits the position

Musket A smoothbore gun

Parliament The government of Great Britain, made up of the king, the House of Lords, the House of Commons, and the prime minister

Partisan An independent fighter not attached to the regular army

Picket Soldiers assigned to guard camps

Powder horn The hollow horn of an ox or cow, fitted with a cover, that soldiers used to carry gunpowder

Privateer A privately owned ship that was authorized by Congress to conduct war

Quarter (as in quartering soldiers): To furnish with shelter, or house

Ramrod A long rod used to push gunpowder and ball down a musket's barrel

Redcoat The nickname for the British soldiers, given to them for their red uniform coats

Redoubt A small fort

Regulars In this case, a reference to the soldiers of the British army

Repeal To take back, revoke

Republic A representative democracy; a type of government in which people exercise power through elected representatives

Sons of Liberty Secret organization founded to protest the Stamp Act

Sovereign (state): Independent of outside authority

Tinderbox A metal box used to hold tinder (cloth or wood) to light a fire, and the flint and steel to ignite it

Tories Loyalist Americans who sided with the Crown

Veto In this case, the president's right to refuse to approve a bill passed by Congress

Volley A simultaneous firing of guns

Whigs Patriot Americans who fought against England

Writs of Assistance Written orders from the British government

A Guide to Officers

Americans/Patriots

Ethan Allen
Benedict Arnold (before 1780)
William Campbell
George Rogers Clark
Horatio Gates
Nathanael Greene
John Paul Jones
Henry Knox
Charles Lee
Henry "Light-Horse Harry" Lee
Benjamin Lincoln
Francis Marion
Richard Montgomery
Daniel Morgan
William Moultrie
Andrew Pickens
William Prescott
Israel Putnam
Philip Schuyler
John Stark
John Sullivan
Thomas Sumter
Artemus Ward
Joseph Warren
George Washington
William Washington
Anthony Wayne

Europeans who Fought on the Side of the Americans

Admiral d'Estaing
Comte de Grasse
Johann de Kalb
Thaddeus Kosciuszko
Marquis de Lafayette
Casimir Pulaski
Comte de Rochambeau
Baron Friedrich von Steuben

British/Redcoats

John André
Benedict Arnold (after 1780)
John Burgoyne
Henry Clinton
Charles Cornwallis
Patrick Ferguson
Thomas Gage
Henry Hamilton
Richard Howe
William Howe
Peter Parker
John Pitcairn
Barry St. Leger
Banastre Tarleton

Biographies

Abigail Adams (1744–1818): Self-taught and spirited Abigail Adams became the nation's second first lady and was a great influence on her husband, John. Their son, John Quincy Adams, was sixth president of the United States.

John Adams (1735–1826): Lawyer, Continental Congress delegate, minister to the Netherlands and Great Britain, John Adams became George Washington's vice president and the second president of the United States.

Samuel Adams (1722–1803): A founder of the Sons of Liberty and delegate at the Continental Congresses, Samuel Adams was a driving force in pushing the colonies toward freedom.

Benedict Arnold (1741–1801): This hero of Forts Ticonderoga and Quebec turned traitor. He gained nothing for his treachery and was hated in both America and England.

John Burgoyne (1722–1792): British general "Gentleman Johnny" Burgoyne failed in his efforts to cut off the New England colonies and surrendered at Saratoga. He had greater success after the war as a playwright in England.

George Rogers Clark (1752–1818): This bold militia leader brought an end to British control and Indian raids in the west. (His younger brother William was co-captain of the Lewis and Clark Expedition.)

General Sir Henry Clinton (1730–1795): Though born in the colonies, Clinton fought the patriots as commander in chief of the British army in North America, replacing Howe in 1778.

Lord Charles Cornwallis (1738–1805): He won many battles, but Cornwallis is most famous for surrendering at Yorktown. After the war, he was appointed governor-general of India.

John Dickinson (1732–1808): Though he at first opposed the rebellion, Dickinson led the committee that drafted the Articles of Confederation and volunteered to fight. He attended the Constitutional Convention and later founded Dickinson College.

Benjamin Franklin (1706–1790): Inventor, scientist, printer, and publisher, Franklin helped draft the Declaration of Independence, won France over to the patriot cause, and was a delegate at the Constitutional Convention.

Horatio Gates (1728–1806): American general Gates's reputation soared at Saratoga, then sank after the defeat at Camden.

George III (1738–1820): King of England during the American Revolution, George III ruled from 1760 to 1820. He was declared unfit, due to mental illness, for the last 10 years of his reign.

Nathanael Greene (1742–1786): Greene, a Rhode Island Quaker, became one of the Continental Army's greatest generals. His remarkable strategies led to the defeat of the British in the South.

Alexander Hamilton (1757–1804): Hamilton served as Washington's wartime aide, as a delegate to the Constitutional Convention, and as treasury secretary of the United States. He was an author of *The Federalist Papers* and a driving force in ratifying the Constitution.

John Hancock (1737–1793): Wealthy trader, Sons of Liberty supporter, and president of the Second Continental Congress, Hancock served nine terms as governor of Massachusetts.

Patrick Henry (1736–1799): A lawyer, Continental Congress delegate, and Virginia's first governor, Henry influenced many with his strong, stirring speeches.

Admiral Lord Richard Howe (1725–1799): Lord Richard led the British forces at sea and was brother to General William Howe.

General Sir William Howe (1729–1814): While commander in chief of the British troops, Howe abandoned Boston, occupied Manhattan, and took Philadelphia. After his service, he was knighted.

John Jay (1745–1829): Jay helped negotiate the Treaty of Paris and was one of the authors of *The Federalist Papers.* He became chief justice of the Supreme Court, then governor of New York.

Thomas Jefferson (1743–1826): Author of the Declaration of Independence, governor of Virginia, minis-

ter to France, George Washington's secretary of state, and the third president of the United States, Jefferson found time to be a scientist, gardener, and architect.

John Paul Jones (1747–1792): This fearless captain of *Bonhomme Richard* was born in Scotland but fought for America, was knighted by French king Louis XVI, and fought in the Russian navy.

Henry Knox (1750–1806): This bookseller-turned-general eventually became secretary of war under President George Washington.

Thaddeus Kosciuszko (1746–1817): Kosciuszko was a Polish military engineer and one of the first foreign volunteers in the American army.

Marquis de Lafayette (1757–1834): This young French nobleman volunteered for the American cause, became Washington's most trusted aide, and played a leading role in the French Revolution, too. His real name? Marie-Joseph-Paul-Yves-Roch-Gilbert du Motier.

Charles Lee (1731–1782): Washington's most senior general, Lee was court-martialed after the Battle of Monmouth and dismissed from the army.

Henry "Light-Horse Harry" Lee (1756–1818): A bold cavalryman who later served as governor of Virginia, Lee was the father of future Civil War general Robert E. Lee.

James Madison (1751–1836): Called the "Father of the Constitution" for his role at the Constitutional

Convention, Madison was an author of *The Federalist Papers,* secretary of state under Jefferson, and the fourth president of the United States.

Francis Marion (1732–1795): "The Swamp Fox" outsmarted the British with shrewd tactics. After the war, he protested the harassment of Tories as a South Carolina state senator.

Joseph Plumb Martin (1760–1850): During his seven-year service in the Continental Army, Martin fought in major battles, suffered at Valley Forge and Morristown, and witnessed the surrender at Yorktown.

George Mason (1725–1792): Mason drafted Virginia's constitution and bill of rights. At the Constitutional Convention, he refused to sign the document without a bill of rights.

Daniel Morgan (1736–1802): Frontiersman Morgan defeated Tarleton's Legion at the Battle of Cowpens. After the war, he served in Congress.

Gouverneur Morris (1752–1816): The one-legged and sharp-witted Morris spoke out often at the Constitutional Convention and shaped the final version of the Constitution.

James Otis (1725–1783): Patriot and lawyer James Otis argued in Massachusetts's court against the writs of assistance and coined the phrase "Taxation without representation is tyranny."

Thomas Paine (1737–1809): Englishman Thomas Paine donated the proceeds of his pamphlet, *Common Sense,* to the cause of his adopted country.

Count Casimir Pulaski (1748–1779): An exiled Polish soldier, Count Pulaski became a cavalry commander in the American army and gave his life for the cause.

Edmund Randolph (1753–1813): Randolph introduced the Virginia Plan at the Constitutional Convention but refused to sign the Constitution. He became attorney general, then secretary of state.

Paul Revere (1734–1818): This silversmith and loyal patriot participated in the Boston Tea Party and made a famous ride when the British marched out of Boston.

Comte de Rochambeau, or **Jean-Baptiste-Donatien de Vimeur** (1725–1807): The commander of the French army in the American Revolutionary War, Rochambeau was imprisoned during France's Reign of Terror and nearly guillotined.

Daniel Shays (1747–1825): A captain during the war, Shays led a rebellion against the Massachusetts government after the war.

Roger Sherman (1721–1793): Sherman signed both the Declaration of Independence and the Constitution. He offered the Connecticut, or Great, Compromise at the Convention.

Baron Friedrich Wilhelm von Steuben (1730–1794): The baron taught and drilled the Americans at Valley Forge until they became a disciplined fighting army. After the war, he became a United States citizen.

Banastre Tarleton (1754–1833): Called "Bloody Ban," "The Butcher," and "Attila" for his cruelty during the war, Tarleton returned to England where he served in Parliament and received a knighthood.

Thayendanegea (Joseph Brant) (1742–1807): A Mohawk chief, Thayendanegea was educated in a colonial school, became a British captain, led attacks against colonists, and took his people to a new home in Canada.

Joseph Warren (1741–1775): Doctor Warren wrote the Suffolk Resolves, helped organize early patriot efforts, and met his death at the Battle of Bunker Hill.

Mercy Otis Warren (1728–1814): Warren was an Anti-Federalist who wrote poems, plays, and a history of the Revolution.

George Washington (1732–1799): A surveyor and planter who became a soldier, a delegate to the Continental Congresses, commander in chief of American forces, and president of the Constitutional Convention, Washington was elected the first president of the United States.

General Anthony Wayne (1745–1796): After the war, "Mad Anthony" Wayne defeated Native Indians at the Battle of Fallen Timbers (in the territory of Ohio). The treaty following opened the Northwest Territory to white settlement.

James Wilson (1742–1798): Wilson, born in Scotland, signed the Declaration of Independence, served in the Continental Congress, wrote Pennsylvania's constitution, argued for a strong central government at the Constitutional Convention, and became a justice of the Supreme Court.

Declaration of Independence

We hold these truths to be self-evident, that all men are created equal, that they are endowed by their Creator with certain unalienable Rights, that among these are Life, Liberty and the pursuit of Happiness.—That to secure these rights, Governments are instituted among Men, deriving their just powers from the consent of the governed,—That whenever any Form of Government becomes destructive of these ends, it is the Right of the People to alter or to abolish it, and to institute new Government, laying its foundation on such principles and organizing its powers in such form, as to them shall seem most likely to effect their Safety and Happiness. Prudence, indeed, will dictate that Governments long established should not be changed for light and transient causes; and accordingly all experience hath shewn, that mankind are more disposed to suffer, while evils are sufferable, than to right themselves by abolishing the forms to which they are accustomed. But when a long train of abuses and usurpations, pursuing invariably the same Object evinces a design to reduce them under absolute Despotism, it is their right, it is their duty, to throw off such Government, and to provide new Guards for their future security.—Such has been the patient sufferance of these Colonies; and such is now the necessity which constrains them to alter their former Systems of Government. The history of the present King of Great Britain is a history of repeated injuries and usurpations, all having in direct object the establishment of an absolute Tyranny over these States. To prove this, let Facts be submitted to a candid world.

He has refused his Assent to Laws, the most wholesome and necessary for the public good.

He has forbidden his Governors to pass Laws of immediate and pressing importance, unless suspended in their operation till his Assent should be obtained; and when so suspended, he has utterly neglected to attend to them.

He has refused to pass other Laws for the accommodation of large districts of people, unless those people would relinquish the right of Representation in the Legislature, a right inestimable to them and formidable to tyrants only.

He has called together legislative bodies at places unusual, uncomfortable, and distant from the depository of their public Records, for the sole purpose of fatiguing them into compliance with his measures.

He has dissolved Representative Houses repeatedly, for opposing with manly firmness his invasions on the rights of the people.

He has refused for a long time, after such dissolutions, to cause others to be elected; whereby the Legislative powers, incapable of Annihilation, have returned to the People at large for their exercise; the State remaining in the mean time exposed to all the dangers of invasion from without, and convulsions within.

He has endeavoured to prevent the population of these States; for that purpose obstructing the Laws for Naturalization of Foreigners; refusing to pass others to encourage their migrations hither, and raising the conditions of new Appropriations of Lands.

He has obstructed the Administration of Justice, by refusing his Assent to Laws for establishing Judiciary powers.

He has made Judges dependent on his Will alone, for the tenure of their offices, and the amount and payment of their salaries.

He has erected a multitude of New Offices, and sent hither swarms of Officers to harrass our people, and eat out their substance.

He has kept among us, in times of peace, Standing Armies without the Consent of our legislatures.

He has affected to render the Military independent of and superior to the Civil power.

He has combined with others to subject us to a jurisdiction foreign to our constitution, and unacknowledged by our laws; giving his Assent to their Acts of pretended Legislation:

For Quartering large bodies of armed troops among us:

For protecting them, by a mock Trial, from punishment for any Murders which they should commit on the Inhabitants of these States:

For cutting off our Trade with all parts of the world:

For imposing Taxes on us without our Consent:

For depriving us in many cases, of the benefits of Trial by Jury:

For transporting us beyond Seas to be tried for pretended offences:

For abolishing the free System of English Laws in a neighbouring Province, establishing therein an Arbitrary government, and enlarging its Boundaries so as to render it at once an example and fit instrument for introducing the same absolute rule into these Colonies:

For taking away our Charters, abolishing our most valuable Laws, and altering fundamentally the Forms of our Governments:

For suspending our own Legislatures, and declaring themselves invested with power to legislate for us in all cases whatsoever.

He has abdicated Government here, by declaring us out of his Protection and waging War against us.

He has plundered our seas, ravaged our Coasts, burnt our towns, and destroyed the lives of our people.

He is at this time transporting large Armies of foreign Mercenaries to compleat the works of death, desolation and tyranny, already begun with circumstances of Cruelty & perfidy scarcely paralleled in the most barbarous ages, and totally unworthy the Head of a civilized nation.

He has constrained our fellow Citizens taken Captive on the high Seas to bear Arms against their Country, to become the executioners of their friends and Brethren, or to fall themselves by their Hands.

He has excited domestic insurrections amongst us, and has endeavoured to bring on the inhabitants of our frontiers, the merciless Indian Savages, whose known rule of warfare, is an undistinguished destruction of all ages, sexes and conditions.

In every stage of these Oppressions We have Petitioned for Redress in the most humble terms: Our repeated Petitions have been answered only by repeated injury. A Prince whose character is thus marked by every act which may define a Tyrant, is unfit to be the ruler of a free people.

Nor have We been wanting in attentions to our Brittish brethren. We have warned them from time to time of attempts by their legislature to extend an unwarrantable jurisdiction over us. We have reminded them of the circumstances of our emigration and settlement here. We have appealed to their native justice and magnanimity, and we have conjured them by the ties of our common kindred to disavow these usurpations, which, would inevitably interrupt our connections and correspondence. They too have been deaf to the voice of justice and of consanguinity. We must, therefore, acquiesce in the necessity, which denounces our Separation, and hold them, as we hold the rest of mankind, Enemies in War, in Peace Friends.

We, therefore, the Representatives of the united States of America, in General Congress, Assembled, appealing to the Supreme Judge of the world for the rectitude of our intentions, do, in the Name, and by Authority of the good People of these Colonies, solemnly publish and declare, That these United Colonies are, and of Right ought to be Free and Independent States; that they are Absolved from all Allegiance to the British Crown, and that all political connection between them and the State of Great Britain, is and ought to be totally dissolved; and that as Free and Independent States, they have full Power to levy War, conclude Peace, contract Alliances, establish Commerce, and to do all other Acts and Things which Independent States may of right do. And for the support of this Declaration, with a firm reliance on the protection of divine Providence, we mutually pledge to each other our Lives, our Fortunes and our sacred Honor.

Georgia:
Button Gwinnett
Lyman Hall
George Walton

North Carolina:
William Hooper
Joseph Hewes
John Penn

South Carolina:
Edward Rutledge
Thomas Heyward, Jr.
Thomas Lynch, Jr.
Arthur Middleton

Massachusetts:
John Hancock

Maryland:
Samuel Chase
William Paca

Thomas Stone
Charles Carroll of
    Carrollton

Virginia:
George Wythe
Richard Henry Lee
Thomas Jefferson
Benjamin Harrison
Thomas Nelson, Jr.
Francis Lightfoot Lee
Carter Braxton

Pennsylvania:
Robert Morris
Benjamin Rush
Benjamin Franklin
John Morton
George Clymer
James Smith
George Taylor

James Wilson
George Ross

Delaware:
Caesar Rodney
George Read
Thomas McKean

New York:
William Floyd
Philip Livingston
Francis Lewis
Lewis Morris

New Jersey:
Richard Stockton
John Witherspoon
Francis Hopkinson
John Hart
Abraham Clark

New Hampshire:
Josiah Bartlett
William Whipple

Massachusetts:
Samuel Adams
John Adams
Robert Treat Paine
Elbridge Gerry

Rhode Island:
Stephen Hopkins
William Ellery

Connecticut:
Roger Sherman
Samuel Huntington
William Williams
Oliver Wolcott

New Hampshire:
Matthew Thornton

Web Sites to Explore

America's Library

www.americaslibrary.gov/cgi-bin/page.cgi

Visit this special Library of Congress site to "Jump Back in Time" and "Meet Amazing Americans."

Ben's Guide to the United States Government

www.bensguide.gpo.gov

What better guide than Ben Franklin to help you understand the ins and outs of the U.S. government? Click on your grade level for best results.

Documents at The National Archives

www.nara.gov/exhall/charters

View the originals! Visit this site to see the Declaration of Independence, the Constitution, and the Bill of Rights. Click on "Founding Fathers" for biographies of the Constitutional Convention delegates.

The House of Representatives

www.house.gov

Keep track of legislation and tour the Capitol from this site. Learn how to contact your representatives at www.house.gov/writerep.

National Park Service Revolutionary War Site

www.nps.gov/revwar

The National Park Service is celebrating the 225th anniversary of the Revolution at this site. Click on "This Date in History," view the time line, and check out special events and links.

POTUS! (Presidents of the United States)

www.ipl.org/ref/POTUS

Here's everything you ever wanted to know about the presidents!

The Senate

www.senate.gov

Enhance your knowledge at "Learning About the Senate." Click on "list by state" to find out how to contact your senator.

The Smithsonian's National Museum of American History

www.americanhistory.si.edu

Can't visit the museum? Go on a virtual tour. Visit the "Not Just for Kids" site for more fun.

The White House

www.whitehouse.gov

Learn about current issues and White House history, and stop by the kids' page at this official White House Web site.

Revolutionary War Sites to Visit

Boston National Historical Park

It all started here! Visit Bunker Hill, the Paul Revere House, the site of the Boston Massacre, and more. 15 State Street, Boston, Massachusetts 02109, 617-242-5642, www.nps.gov/bost

Colonial National Historical Park

Imagine the bombardment of Yorktown as you inspect earthworks and 18th-century buildings. (The surrender is reenacted here every October 19th.) P.O. Box 210, Yorktown, VA 23690-0210, 757-898-2410, www.nps.gov/colo

Cowpens National Battlefield

Walk the battlefield to see how Daniel Morgan beat "Bloody Ban" Tarleton. P.O. Box 308, Chesnee, South Carolina 29323, 864-461-2828, www.nps.gov/cowp

Fort Moultrie National Monument

Patriots defended Charleston from this fort's palmetto log walls. 1214 Middle Street, Sullivans Island, South Carolina 29482, 843-883-3123, www.nps.gov/fomo

Fort Stanwix

Witness military drills and musket demonstrations at this 18th-century fort and enter the kids' "soldier for a day" program. 112 East Park Street, Rome, New York 13440, 315-336-2090, www.nps.gov/fost

Fort Ticonderoga National Historic Landmark

Built during the French and Indian War, Fort Ticonderoga was a key site during the Revolution. The museum features 18th-century artillery and uniforms. P.O. Box 390, Ticonderoga, New York 12833, 518-585-2821, www.fort-ticonderoga.org

George Rogers Clark National Historical Park

Learn about Clark's historic march and capture of western forts. 401 South Second Street, Vincennes, Indiana 47591, 812-882-1776, www.nps.gov/gero

Guilford Courthouse National Military Park

Inspect both patriot and British positions to understand and relive a battle that changed the war. 2332 New Garden Road, Greensboro, North Carolina 27410, 336-288-1776, www.nps.gov/guco

Independence National Historical Park

Independence Hall (formerly the State House) looks just as it did during the hot summer of the Constitutional Convention. See the Liberty Bell and the home where Jefferson wrote the Declaration of Independence, too. 313 Walnut Street, Philadelphia, Pennsylvania 19106, 215-597-8974, www.nps.gov/inde

Kings Mountain National Military Park

Visit the site where angry overmountain men defeated British soldiers. P.O. Box 40, Kings Mountain, North Carolina 28086, 864-936-7921, www.nps.gov/kimo

Minute Man National Historical Park

Follow the Battle Road Trail near Lexington and Concord where the first shots of war rang out. 174 Liberty Street, Concord, Massachusetts 01742, 978-369-6993 x22, www.nps.gov/mima

Monticello

The home Thomas Jefferson designed and built is filled with artifacts, books, and inventions. P.O. Box 217, Charlottesville, Virginia 22902, 804-984-9822, www.monticello.org

Moores Creek National Battlefield

Broadswords rang and bagpipes played during the battle here. Walk the history trail near Widow Moore's Creek. 40 Patriots Hall Drive, Currie, North Carolina 28435, 910-283-5591, www.nps.gov/mocr

Morristown National Historical Park

Explore Washington's headquarters and reconstructed soldier huts. Morristown's living history programs show how American soldiers lived. Washington Place, Morristown, New Jersey 07960, 973-539-2085, www.nps.gov/morr

Mount Vernon Estate & Gardens

Workers in period costumes bring George Washington's home to life. 703-780-2000, www.mountvernon.org

Ninety Six National Historic Site

Ninety Six's star fort was held under siege by Nathanael Greene's patriot troops. P.O. Box 496, Ninety Six, South Carolina 29666, 864-543-4068, www.nps.gov/nisi

The Old Barracks Museum

Once an 18th-century quarters, hospital, and prison, today this museum features interesting exhibits and a summer day camp for kids. 1758 Barrack Street, Trenton, New Jersey 18608, 609-396-1776, www.barracks.org

Overmountain Victory National Historic Trail

Not a park but a trail, this 300-mile path honors the overmountain men. Every year, reenactors remember their deeds. Atlanta Federal Center, 100 Alabama Street, SW, Atlanta, Georgia 30303, 404-562-3124, www.nps.gov/ovvi

Saratoga National Historical Park

Military encampments, colonial demonstrations, and costumed guides bring 1777 back to life. (See a monument dedicated to Benedict Arnold's leg!) 648 Route 32, Stillwater, New York 12170-1604, 518-664-9821, www.nps.gov/sara

The Smithsonian's National Museum of American History

Three floors of American history include a Hands On History Room, exhibits on the American Presidency and the First Ladies, and the original Star-Spangled Banner. 14th Street and Constitution Avenue NW, Washington, DC 20560 202-357-2700, www.americanhistory.si.edu

Valley Forge National Historic Park

Meet soldiers in period dress, explore log huts, and learn how American soldiers survived a bleak winter. P.O. Box 953, Valley Forge, Pennsylvania 19482, 610-783-1077, www.nps.gov/vafo

Washington Crossing State Park

Washington made his famous crossing of the Delaware River here. 355 Washington Crossing-Pennington Road, Titusville, New Jersey 08560, 609-737-0623, www.state.nj.us/dep/forestry/parks/washcros.htm

Bibliography

Bobrick, Benson. *Angel in the Whirlwind: The Triumph of the American Revolution.* New York: Penguin Books, 1997.

Bowen, Catherine Drinker. *Miracle at Philadelphia: The Story of the Constitutional Convention May to September 1787.* Boston: Little, Brown and Company, 1986.

The Editors of Time-Life Books. *The American Story: The Revolutionaries.* Alexandria, Virginia: Time-Life Books, 1996.

Feinberg, Barbara Silberdick. *Constitutional Amendments.* New York: Henry Holt and Company, 1996.

Franklin, Benjamin. *Franklin: Writings.* New York: Library of America, 1987.

Glubok, Shirley. *Home and Child Life in Colonial Days.* Toronto, Ontario: The Macmillan Company, 1969.

Jackson, Kennell. *America Is Me: The Most Asked and Least Understood Questions About Black American History.* New York: HarperPerennial, 1997.

Langguth, A. J. *Patriots: The Men Who Started the American Revolution.* New York: Simon & Schuster, Inc., 1988.

Meltzer, Milton, editor. *The American Revolutionaries: A History in Their Own Words 1750–1800.* New York: Thomas Y. Crowell Publishers, 1987.

*Tunis, Edwin. *Colonial Living.* New York: Thomas Y. Crowell Company, 1957.

*Tunis, Edwin. *The Young United States: 1783 to 1830.* New York: World Publishing Company, 1969.

Wilbur, C. Keith. *The Revolutionary Soldier: 1775–1783.* Philadelphia: Chelsea House Publishers, 1997.

The following books and the books marked with a * above are recommended for younger readers:

Brenner, Barbara. *If You Were There in 1776.* New York: Macmillan Publishing Company, 1994.

Forbes, Esther. *Johnny Tremain.* New York: Bantam Doubleday Dell Books, 1971.

Ritchie, Donald A. *Know Your Government: The U.S. Constitution.* Philadelphia: Chelsea House Publishers, 1989.

Scheer, George F., editor. *Joseph Plumb Martin: Yankee Doodle Boy.* New York: William R. Scott, Inc., 1964.

Sobol, Donald J. *Lock, Stock, and Barrel.* Philadelphia: The Westminster Press, 1965.

Index

Other children's activity books by Janis Herbert

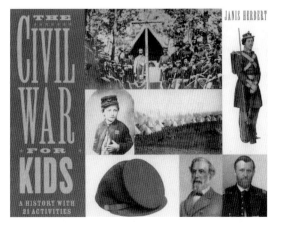

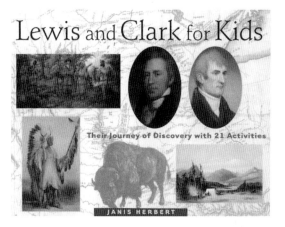

Leonardo da Vinci for Kids: His Life and Ideas, 21 Activities

"A lively biography of the ultimate Renaissance man. Herbert describes Leonardo's life while also providing a good deal of historical information about art."—*School Library Journal*

"Thoroughly illustrated and well designed, this is a fine purchase that rises above the current bounty of available books on the subject."—*Booklist*

The Civil War for Kids: A History with 21 Activities

"For children who *really* want to know what it felt like to take an active role in the past, *The Civil War for Kids* is *it!*"
—*Civil War Book Review*

"Teachers and parents will find this book a very handy tool to help teach their students and children about this critical period in our nation's history."
—D. Scott Hartwig, Historian, Gettysburg, Pennsylvania

Lewis and Clark for Kids: Their Journey of Discovery with 21 Activities

"The Lewis and Clark expedition was not only one of America's greatest adventures, it was one of our nation's greatest leaps in learning. Geography, ethnology, zoology, botany, and literature—the Corps of Discovery made important contributions to them all. This book invites readers to join Lewis and Clark's epic journey and helps them make their own discoveries along the way."—Dayton Duncan, author of *Out West: American Journey Along the Lewis and Clark Trail*